Energize Your Creative Super Powers

7 Ways to Spiritual Fitness

Cath DePalma

A Companion Workbook to
*I Can Do This Thing Called Life:
And So Can You!*

WiseWoman
Press

Energize Your Creative Super Powers: 7 Ways to Spiritual Fitness
© 2020 by Cath DePalma

A COMPANION WORKBOOK TO *I CAN DO THIS THING CALLED LIFE: AND SO CAN YOU!*

Published by WiseWoman Press
Vancouver, Washington
www.wisewomanpress.com

ISBN: 978-0-945385-36-3

This workbook belongs to:

_____

My intention is to experience:

_____

_____

Signed: _____

Date:_____

Dedication

This book is dedicated to my magnificent kids... each one a universe of wonder and awesome in themselves. Each are so different from the others and yet so pure, sweet and good. They are my lifesavers, teaching me by example what it's like to be youthful again, energetic, high-minded, determined, creative and loving whenever I forget to see myself that way. Each one of them, in their own special way, gives me something no one else can.

One year my oldest son, Nick (about 13 at the time) and my daughter, Liz (who was about 10), walked to a nearby toy store and bought wrapping paper with thousand-dollar bills printed on it. They cut out the bills and placed them all over the house. Imagine my surprise as I walked in, amazed. At the time I hadn't been feeling particularly prosperous. I had just left a well-paying job in Atlanta and moved to Florida to start my ministry. They said they were helping me get used to having money. I will cherish that moment and others forever.

Joseph, the baby, who is 15 years younger than Liz, challenged me even more. How can you say *no* to a spirit that knows exactly what he wants? I just had to get with the plan and figure out ways to support him with his dreams. My children have been my greatest teachers, pushing me into being more of my real self. I am extremely blessed.

Contents

Foreword

Michael Nichols, 26 years into his sentence in the Missouri State Penitentiary, wrote:

There was a time in my life when I didn't really understand the concept of death. I didn't understand the enormity of the pain of loss to children when parents get snatched away or the devastation of a parent who loses a child, until I lost my own.

I didn't understand the ripple effect in a community, or the tragedy of a life cut short. I didn't appreciate my own life, I didn't value that life. I could not fully understand the value of another human life as I couldn't understand my own. Yet throughout the many moons of my incarceration I came to understand the devastation of my crime.

I've ruined lives, including my own, yet I know that what is done in the past can never be changed; but people who have done many negative things in the past can change.

Today, I am a loving person and understanding and patient. I have grown, I have redeemed myself. I have rehabilitated not with the expectation of a parole date but in the process of healing, purging the poison of ignorance and self-hate. I have become a role model for many of the younger generations.

I, myself, am a shining example that people can change, and that no matter one's background, nor their past actions, there is no such thing as a [throwaway] child.

Reverend Cath DePalma, your book, I Can Do This Thing Called Life and So Can You!, really gave me a chance to reflect on life in general. All the truths that I have learned and embraced I now apply and teach. The way you applied the teachings to your daily life with family and friends is a

i

beauty I, too, wish to emulate. The thing I do know I will accomplish more than anything else, will be that my family and friends will never have to set foot into this world in which I now dwell.

I thank you for sending me your book. I have taken notes from it and added it into my studies.

Michael

As of 2018, Michael has achieved honor status, and moved to the Enhanced Care Unit where he lives and works, helping prisoners with medical conditions as a Daily Living Assistant. He continues to take classes to better himself and is currently writing his own book on spirituality.

Preface

This book is a handbook of practical applications to help the reader have a deeper connection and see more meaning in their life. Spiritual practices are a way to shift our perceptions and awareness so that we can experience the new. When I started on this path years ago, I was led to begin using some of these practices myself. I began to change my mind, and keep it changed. That made all the difference. I began seeing definite changes for the better in my life. This inspired me to do more. How could I stop when my life continued to improve as I took control of myself and my life? I quickly came to the realization that my desiring nature was good, and that in an infinite Universe I really could expect more.

Having good ideas isn't enough and can only take us so far. Thinking beautiful, new, expansive ideas needs to be put to work for us. Thinking them is only the first step. If they don't change us permanently and continue to make our lives better, make us feel better about ourselves, or make our lives more to our liking, they're not fitting the bill as to what is possible. There is a way to make them work for us in the creation of new and improved life experiences.

Like exercising our bodies, we must keep at it. We can't stop working out for long without our muscles losing their strength. Spiritual workouts are a lifelong commitment and the payoff is more than generous, with plenty of surprises. Strengthening our spiritual muscles is a gift we give ourselves that keeps on giving. For as long as we continue to choose to do what we can to grow in spiritual strength, we will be pleasantly surprised at the new "us" that emerges. We can look forward to an even better "us"! I have heard someone say, "Muscle is the new medicine." Spiritual muscle is definitely the "medicine " for everything we will ever face.

Introduction

Hurricane season in Florida is between June and November each year. Usually, not much happens. A couple of years ago there was no doubt huge storms were brewing. My husband, John, and I had had been putting off having some tree work done, including having a dead tree removed. That year we knew instinctively it was time to take care of our trees.

When our son came home from college that summer, we considered replacing some sections of our wood fence that were rotted and loose (and could cause damage if blown around by hurricane-force winds). It is so easy to put off a job like that during humid, 95-degree heat, but since I wouldn't be the one doing the work, I couldn't make the decision. I did mention that there is never a good time—hot, humid weather, rainy season, don't feel like doing it, someday we'll do it—which may have helped the guys decide to take it on.

We also had some unexpected plumbing work completed earlier that year (which gave others a problem during and after the storm, and kept some people out of their homes for even longer).All this work on our home would make a difference for us in the days to come.

Just before Hurricane Irma made landfall, John boarded up three large windows (which was a first in our 24 years in Central Florida).Were there other things that we needed to do, like putting on a new roof? That wasn't going to happen this year. Of course, there are always things that need to be updated and replaced in a 30-year-old house. We did what we could and then we just had to trust. It helped to have experienced major hurricanes before. We had become familiar with what needed to be done to protect ourselves. Getting those tasks done, along with our spiritual work, allowed us to know we were safe and protected and gave us the assurance that we had done what we could to prepare, and it would have to be enough.

v

The evening before the hurricane hit our area; we had a nice dinner, a glass of wine, and watched a movie. We weren't thinking this might be the last supper. It was nothing like that. We were as calm, cool and collected as we could be. I did have a *moment* about midnight, when the weatherman brought up the possibility of tornadoes coming our way as well. I looked around and thought to myself, *I have nothing packed!* My important belongings were spread out all over the house. I decided to spend a few minutes gathering those things I absolutely couldn't live without, so that I could grab them quickly if it became necessary. It was a great exercise in seeing how little I really needed and how much I could walk away from. I passed the test on attachment to stuff!

Next, I went to bed and fell into a half sleep. I was able to hear the wind, smaller branches falling on the roof, and even a big thump somewhere in the neighborhood (which must have been the huge old oak tree that fell across the road a few houses down from us). There was nothing else to do but know we were divinely protected.

Morning came, and the winds continued to blow but with a little less ferocity than before. Finally, we had a clear view of our home and yard. We stepped outside to get a quick assessment, thrilled to have made it through the night with our home intact. Thank you, God! We had no complaints. Even though there were two days of yard cleanup, the small inconveniences we encountered were nothing compared to what others had to go through. If it meant we had to wait longer to have electricity restored because someone else needed it more, so be it. We were okay with waiting. It was all a great spiritual practice. Excellent "Peaceful Warrior" training.

To help me keep the greater perspective, I had just purchased the books, *The Book of Joy* and *The Places that Scare You*. The Dalai Lama, Desmond Tutu and Pema Chodron, as well as John all kept me company and in check. I could not have asked for better companions.

Just weeks before we all had witnessed Hurricane Harvey and the destruction it left in Houston. Days before this, my son Nick called, disheartened that his neighborhood in Portland, Oregon, was covered in ashes from the fires in the Columbia River Gorge. Devastating events continued around the globe.

What were we to think? How does one handle unsettling news and keep one's center? It was hard not to see others as well as ourselves as victims in a world gone out of control. It was even more difficult to see that prayers *were* making a difference. We surely do not need to know what things would have been like without them.

From my limited perspective I saw so much good come out of this. Only a week before, people were crazed, stocking up on food, gas, batteries and water. But afterward, things calmed down. Of course, there were some harsh realities for some to face, but we all felt a huge sigh of relief that it was over. Facing the facts is easier than facing the unknown. The fear of what might happen was gone.

John and I got to know our next-door neighbors: a young couple, their small child and new baby. Normally they were quiet and kept to themselves. Now, friendlier contact was made as they needed advice, being first-time homeowners facing a category three hurricane. One day, after they had left their home to stay with family, a huge birthday present for their son arrived at their doorstep. We were able to take care of that for them. When our electricity came on, I was able to text them with the question, "Are you ready to come home?" They were so excited!

Kids were out on the streets, happily running around, playing and riding their bikes and skateboards. They had to be creative without their usual "go to's"--phones, TVs and video games.

Neighbors were out on the street, talking to each other and comparing experiences. The sound of people filled the air. I have to say, I felt an aliveness in our neighborhood that I hadn't felt since the last hurricane came through years ago. People everywhere were engaging in conversation, sharing their experiences and ideas about recovering from the storm.

One of our neighbors had to face her worst nightmare, her fear of not being in control, plus had to leave her home while we waited almost nine days for electricity (which now seems like nothing compared to what others experienced, especially in Puerto Rico). These were some big lessons in surrender and trust.

Addictions, appetites and habits had to be faced by us all. In the aftermath of the storm, priorities had to be established. Everything else fell by the wayside. We were fully immersed in the business of living, and it was invigorating! Without escapism, we automatically were more present. Without all the distractions of electronic communication, I found I could be even more observant of my own thoughts. I couldn't see that I missed out on anything, really, except more news about the disaster and the regular checking of my phone. It was as if a giant reset button had been pushed for our world. With normal living put to a halt, I felt a peace and clarity that I haven't always had.

How can I say these things were bad? I cannot. I don't believe we were ever meant to be so tied down, in such control, and living small. Life is about growth and expansion. In situations like the one I just described, we are all asked to get up to speed with our own inner being. That is where our true strength lies.

Somehow every one of our needs was met. I was blessed to be invited to a friend's house for a few nights of sleep in air conditioning. Also, a few warm showers were a nice break from all the cold ones!

In the middle of it all, we had a very nice visit from our good friend, Rev. Dr. Bob Deen, who had come to work with our community and would later speak at a retreat nearby. We had time to relax, play and enjoy different restaurants that were opening back up. It was heartwarming to host a friend and colleague (whom we have known for close to 30 years) and spend quality time with him, just hanging out. I even got to try my first Vietnamese food. Yum! It was almost as if we were living an alternate reality (no electricity at the house and cool, air-conditioned restaurants with delicious foods to experience).

At the end of our power outage, I was able to get in touch with a good friend who was anxiously waiting to hear how we did, complete with all the juicy details and my perspective on things. Her family and friend wanted to know if we evacuated, and if we didn't, why not? All I can say is that John and I both followed our internal guidance. If there had been a reason to leave, we would have known. We hadn't sensed the message to get out, so we stayed.

What can we all do to better prepare ourselves for challenges such as this?

Here are some questions I had to ask myself in the middle of it all:

1) Do we have to have hurricanes and storms to get our attention back to what we really need, to help us live in a way that feeds our souls?

2) Are we prepared, mentally and spiritually, to face whatever difficulties come our way?

3) Are we present to the ways in which Spirit prepares us for an upcoming event, internally and externally? Are we present to how Spirit prepares us continuously for life in general? Are we taking the necessary steps we are led to take? If not, why not?

4) Are we present to the ways in which Spirit is there for us all the time? Are we present to how much love and extreme support there really is?

5) How attached are we to our stuff, our material goods or to being in control and having our way?

A couple of other questions we must ask ourselves personally are:

1) How much of this upheaval are *we* creating by watching all these doomsday movies, by not facing our fears and getting help with them, or by not growing?

2) How much of what is happening have we contributed to with our own anger, fear and frustration?

What can we do?

We can do our spiritual practices. They are the greatest survival tool we have. Without them we don't stand a chance. I can't say enough about what mine mean to me and the difference they make in my life. I can't say where I would be without them.

We can stop getting caught up in the drama and feeling sorry for people who are going through things. We can compassionately know that none of us is ever alone. We are perfectly supported, and the opportunities before us are *for* us, in ways we may not know, to the degree that we are open and receptive to them. There is a richness to even the most horrendous of situations if we look at it that way and see that for each other when we can't see it for ourselves.

For the fun of it, I looked up the meaning of the hurricane's name, Irma. It means noble, universal and even "war goddess." I have to say, the "Goddess" did a great job of cleaning us out on so many levels. Whether we can see that as good or not depends on where we are with ourselves and our views on life. She played her part in the universal scheme of things.

In the end, it was my desperate neighbor (who had worked herself up into such a tizzy before the storm that she was admitted to the hospital for a couple of days afterward) that sought out the place where the energy workers took their morning break. She had had enough, and she informed them that our portion of the neighborhood was *still* without electricity. (Notice I am not saying we were without power because we weren't!)

Within 20 minutes of her conversation the neighborhood was back to normal. She needed that win. That demonstration showed me how much every single person serves their purpose and how important it is that we don't write them out of the script. I am sure none of us are the same as we were before the storm hit. I pray we keep it that way and don't slip back into complacency by remembering what is truly important. We are all being called to a higher order of being by divine design. It's time to stop avoiding our destiny and become all that we came here to be. We always get what we need!

For a job well done, the Universe, as my husband, had a dozen roses sent to me the day after our electricity was restored with a note saying: "To the best hurricane buddy ever! I love you! John." After 27 years together, I would say we are doing extremely well. I could not have handled any of it very well without my years of spiritual training and practice.

P.S. If this is how Spiritual Practices help with emergencies, imagine how powerfully they help when things are going well!

Cath DePalma

Special Notes to My Readers

1. Throughout the book, I use different names for God. Here is a list of some of my favorite references to God

Source	Love & Law
Spirit	Energy
Universe	Universal Mind
Infinite Intelligence	Presence
The Tao	Higher Power
Cosmic Intelligence	IT
Life	The Thing Itself
Good	Principle
Truth	The Infinite

One name hardly describes the Ultimate Thing Itself. While most people recognize the word *God*, there are probably as many different interpretations of what God is as there are people. God is beyond names, really. Sometimes I refer to our Source as IT, not out of disrespect in any way, but to get us to expand our idea of God as a personality. Personality implies that God, like us, has an ego, limitations, moods and judgment calls, and explains why we feel that God works for us sometimes but not other times.

We can still have a personal relationship with our God, whatever name we use and feel a connection with, in the midst of ITs impersonalness.

Love and Law are the two aspects we want to remember. Both are aspects of God, Spirit, Life. For a fuller and more comprehensive understanding of what our Source is (at least more than what we are currently seeing), it is important to not limit ourselves to either one...a God of Love or a God of Law. Both sides need to be taken into consideration. This way we know we are *all* loved and are *all* treated fairly and supported, even if we don't quite understand all the laws of the Universe yet.

The God we are talking about goes beyond anything we can imagine, yet it is up to us to stretch our minds to a larger concept of what IT is so we can become more god-like and work alongside this Creative Intelligence...as a partner.

This Intelligence, this Divine and Perfect Love, will respond to us in a way we can relate to and that allows us to feel a connection to IT. We can each have an up-close and personal relationship with our Source, which is always available to us because IT is closer than our very breath.

2. This workbook is for YOU!

I highly recommend reading through the entire book first to become familiar with the different ways to incorporate more spirituality into our lives. I know some readers will be ready to dive into an exercise right away. Some already have a spiritual practice and are looking for ways to go deeper. Others are brand new to this idea and just getting started. Either way, this book is for everyone! Reading the entire book is life changing in itself. From our new place we can begin to take steps and make choices from the selections here that are even more perfect for our individual situations. We may even create some of our own exercises and use this material as a jumping-off place.

Of course, there will be those readers who can't help themselves and want to dive in right away. That is okay, too. We must each listen to our inner guide, as it knows us best. It knows what is right for each of us.

Remember, this is a lifelong process. Introducing new ideas and outlooks requires big adjustments in us. There is no reason to hurry. Part of the journey is being kinder and more loving to ourselves, even if we call it a workout. We can be as lighthearted as we can be and enjoy the process!

Section I

Getting Ready

Concept 1: Our Spiritual Path

We are the guests of an invisible Host whose presence we feel and whose form we shall see when our eyes are opened to the fact that it clothes itself in innumerable forms. It is our business to unite, not to divide; to include, not to exclude; to accept and not to renounce.
~ Ernest Holmes

There are stages to our spiritual growth and expansion. Often, they come step by step. Other times they come all at once. Life is a series of becoming the divine human. Learning is a continual process that reveals more of our true, free and wonderful self. Learning and exploring our surroundings and experiencing more happiness in all we do is not limited or defined by age or formal education. The Universe is continually working with us to be more.

To get a better idea of what that looks like, we could liken our process of transformation to that of the caterpillar becoming a butterfly. There appears to be two main parts to our spiritual unfoldment: a caterpillar-like stage and a transformational stage. Just like a caterpillar fattening up on everything in its path in preparation for the big meltdown and transfiguration that takes place in the chrysalis, when we are ready to get more out of life we are attracted to everything we can get our hands on to read, listen to or study. This is the stage where we are insatiable and can't get enough. We can't help but be excited about the whole new world we have discovered. Taking in a lot of information gets us to a point where we can begin to put together a picture, a new belief system for ourselves, a new frame of reference...one that makes sense to us in our newly evolved state. Even though this is a critical and very essential stage, it is only the beginning. We are only skimming the surface of what is possible and have no idea where this new path will lead.

Eventually we reach a point of saturation, which is a pivotal point for deciding if we are going to move forward. Since we are not caterpillars, we have a choice to either stay with the process or bow out and catch our breath. We may even find this new way of living requires much more of us than we are ready to invest at the present time. That's okay, too.

In order to reap the full benefit of what we've initiated, we must continue on to the second major stage of our spiritual development: a new order of being. If we quit now and say, "I've tried, and it doesn't work," we have not reached the place where we have learned to successfully apply the many fabulous principles that have caught our attention.

This next phase is not for the faint of heart: transfiguration. During this phase our world is—or may appear to be—turned upside down. We may feel like we no longer know which end is up. We seem to lose control of things on the surface as our core strengthens. Major reorientation and reorganization are taking place, and what happens within us must take place outside of us. Major shifts, like the end of a relationship, a new job or health challenge, take place as the result of our taking in this new information. Integration is taking place on all levels of our being that then plays out in our lives. It can be a scary thing if we don't understand what is going on. Indeed, a metamorphosis is taking place.

Whether we delay the process or move forward with it, eventually there does come the point when we are ready to take things deeper, to take our spirituality more seriously. Some have said it was easier when they didn't know anything, but once we get a taste of something better, we want more. Thriving, prospering and growing are in our DNA, part of our divine nature. Once our thought has been expanded, we can't go back to the way we were. Working on our spirituality helps us to feel better and get more satisfaction out of life. It really is about taking personal responsibility for ourselves and the way we live. As we continue to put more effort into bettering ourselves, our lives will take on a whole new look. Just like the magnificent butterfly, free to fly, we emerge from our transformation/transfiguration feeling as though we have come home to our real selves! It is a feeling like no other!

Just like the actual process described above, this book isn't a quick read, or something to superficially skip through. It's not about zooming through the material. There is plenty of material out there to give us short-term enjoyment. I recommend taking it slow and doing a little at a time. This is meant as a handbook to help us get to know ourselves in a more intimate way. It's better to read a section in the chapter and then reflect on our own lives. Even though some of the stories are mine, this course is about the reader. If we take our time, giving ourselves the gift of being with ourselves, we will see how we can go to new depths with our spirituality. We can enjoy ourselves and begin to make this area of our lives more playful. This is about getting to know ourselves spiritually and getting to know the Universe.

Most of us need to do less and be more to appreciate who we are.

Personal Journal Notes

_____

_____

_____

_____

_____

_____

_____

_____

_____

_____

_____

Concept 2: We Are Already WHOLE

What lies behind us and what lies before us are tiny matters compared to what lies within us.

~ Oliver Wendell Holmes

Sometimes we have trouble seeing the whole picture of what is possible for our lives. Maybe we see some of it. Some parts of it are very clear and feel good because we've already accomplished them or see that they are within our reach. Other parts, not as much. We see them as possibilities for someone else, or maybe for another lifetime. It's hard to imagine what *that* life could look like. Our attempts in that direction seem futile and we don't seem to get anywhere. We resort to thinking that maybe it's not to be.

I am pretty sure that I'm not the only one who has ever had this thought. In fact, it took me years of trying to figure out what was wrong with me to discover what one observant visitor could see very plainly.

At the beginning of my ministry, a visiting minister from Canada stayed at our house. He was doing a workshop for our spiritual community. I don't even remember what it was now. I do know this motorcycling preacher knew how to "call things as they are," and before he left, he let me have it in as nice of a way as *he* could. I wanted to know what that "thing" was that was getting in my way, and at the same time, I didn't. I was afraid to face it, but it was obvious to him and he had no trouble blurting out, "I know exactly what your thing is: You don't believe you are *supported*." Ouch! Okay, that stung, but it was quickly over. It was most certainly true. That was it. I don't think he would have left without saying it, and thank God, someone had the clarity and the guts to say it like it is! Now I could do something about it.

Much about my life before this time didn't feel like support. I could come up with plenty of examples of how I have not felt supported throughout my life, beginning with having to move over for a new baby brother before I was a year old, and new siblings arrived on the scene every couple of years after that (there were five of us). I grew up fast and became independent early. Was that a bad thing? Not really. Even though there were plenty of ways I was supported, this was an underlying feeling I carried unknowingly. Later I would learn that support often comes in many different forms and that most people can come up with plenty of examples of how they haven't been supported in their lives if they want to build a case.

The observation that minister had shared led me to an even tougher realization. At the core of my personality self, I didn't believe that I was *enough*. Not feeling enough would, of course, attract not feeling supported. This idea had a sting to it as well. I could feel it at heart level...in my heart chakra.[1] I soon discovered that this spiritual path required courage to face the difficult places in myself that needed healing. It took years of work to get to a place where I know I am enough, that I am already whole. In fact, I was born that way. We all were born that way. Operating from this new place made it easier for me to attract the love and support I needed. In fact, as my self-esteem grew, I learned I had a right to it.

If it is true that we are born whole, why do we feel so incomplete? How can we say we were created by an Infinite Creator, or created in the image and likeness of God, and yet feel so...*not* like a unique and magnificent creation of the Infinite, or *not* like the image and likeness of God at times? (Depending on one's view of God, that could be a good thing, or a not-so-good thing. Here we are talking about a God that is Love.) What is going on?

We don't have to look far in this world to see that we are bombarded with plenty of messages that tell us we need some product, some person in our lives to make us feel complete, something more than what we currently have, or something... whatever it is. We are bombarded by an infinite number of mes-

---

[1] Chakras are centers of spiritual power or energy in the body. According to Indian thought, there are seven main chakras, one of which is the heart.

sages that say we need medication to feel complete and live healthfully. Every commercial is "loaded for bear" to appeal to our sense of "less than" so we will buy their product. It's their business to do so. I am sure there is another way to accomplish the advertisers' goals that doesn't cause us to feel inadequate without their product.

In addition, there are plenty of others in our lives who are not feeling complete, or not feeling like they are enough, who can appear to be working against us. They are not in a place where they can help someone else when they themselves have not felt sufficiently loved and provided for.

Either way, our experience leaves us feeling as if we are not enough, which in Reality cannot be the Truth about us. It's easy to see how our spirit may be perfect. Yet it's hard seeing our human aspects in the way that God, the Infinite, or Love sees us. How does a perfect, loving Creator see ITs creations? God can only see us with eyes of Love, because that is what IT is. That means IT sees us as perfection, as whole, as complete—just the way we are. How about adorable? Yes, that too!

We long to be seen for who we really are. We yearn for it. We long to be seen just as Love sees us. We think maybe some-day, somehow, we will see ourselves that way. We put off for a later date that which is within our reach. Why put off what we can experience today? What about now?

What about seeing ourselves as perfect, whole and com-plete right here and now, with the full benefits of being an actu-alized being and inheriting all the gifts that were meant for us to enjoy?

- What would happen if we believed we were love... total love?
- What would happen if we saw ourselves as good... all the time?
- What would happen if we truly believed that we were creat-ed by a magnificent Creator, or an Intelligence that could only ever create perfection?
- What kind of lies have we been taught and lived with all these years that say we are poor, sick, weak and unhappy?

- What kind of life could be experienced and enjoyed if we were operating from believing the truth about ourselves and our divine nature?

WOW! The possibilities are endless!

When we see ourselves as anything less than the wholeness and perfection that we are, we will experience an incomplete sense of ourselves and a less-than-adequate life experience to match our picture of ourselves, always seeking and searching for more. We will only get more of what we already have or more of what we have always experienced until now if we don't change how we see ourselves and what we believe. Good...and yet, not quite good enough. No amount of money, no amount of love, no amount of good will satisfy us when we aren't feeling true to ourselves—the selves we were created to be.

- What would happen if, instead of believing we would be complete with a degree or promotion, we believed we are complete today, just as we are, as a perfect creation of God?
- What if we stopped seeing ourselves as a failure and looking back on what we've missed out or lost?
- What if we believed that there are never losses, only something greater to be gained?
- What if we believed we already are more than enough to handle whatever is before us?
- What if we believed we already are "more than enough spirit" than is needed to turn our life around and create the life of our dreams?
- What if the whole human race believed that we are more than enough to turn this world around...that no matter what is happening or not happening, there is more than enough love, intelligence, wholesomeness and healthiness about us to make the right decisions for the greater good of all, including for the planet?

The incompleteness we see in our world is merely a reflection of our own beliefs about ourselves. Why wouldn't we see inadequacies all around us if we are seeing ourselves that way? The outer world always reflects the inner one.

As soon as we see from the place of our being whole, we will see that there is more than enough heart, mind, mental ability, intelligence, love, resources and good to turn us around...more than enough good people in the world to enjoy!

Getting to the heart of things is key to helping us move forward. Building our spiritual muscles helps us know we are enough just as we are. We are created to live a rich existence here, and that begins with our having a greater appreciation of who we are. Spiritual practices are a way for us to exercise our spiritual muscles so we can live more richly and fully. They can take us to places we didn't know existed. Once we start down this path, our lives are changed forever. We are not the same person we once were.

Now that I know what spiritual practices can do, I wouldn't give them up for the world. They have done wonders for me! They are a lifeline to a greater existence. Spirituality has always been here for us to access. Now we have specific ways to get in touch with the real Source of our lives. As we grow familiar with them and they become a key part of our lives, we feel better so that we can have a much brighter outlook on life no matter what is going on around us.

Personal Journal Notes

_____

_____

_____

_____

_____

_____

_____

Concept 3: Multidimensional Beings

When you are inspired by some great purpose, some extraordinary project, all your thoughts break their bonds; your mind transcends limitations, and your consciousness expands in every direction, and you find yourself in a new, great and wonderful world.

Dormant forces, faculties and talents become alive, and you discover yourself to be a greater person by far than you ever dreamed yourself to be.

~ Pantanjali (ca. First to Third Century B.C.)

We really are living in a multidimensional Universe, whether we see the world this way or not. Even though it appears that we are living in three dimensions, there are more, making us multidimensional beings. There is more to the world than what we see, and most definitely, more to us than we know. As we go through life, we begin to see that living in the world as we know it can only take us so far. We find ourselves asking, "Is this all there is?" We need more. It's difficult to feel adequate and knowledgeable when we don't have all the pieces to the puzzle. Clearly, we do not have knowledge of the entire playing field that is available to us. We need to know more in order to live successfully. We must avail ourselves of the greater Reality that exists. There is so much more going on than what we can see, hear, taste, touch and feel. As wonderful as it is to experience the delightful world of our senses, there is more here to enjoy than most of us were brought up believing. For us to move into the field of infinite possibilities, we must break out of the paradigm in which we have been operating. Embracing the idea that there is more behind the scenes yet to be revealed begins to open new doors that were not available to us before. Beyond the physical lies the nonphysical, or metaphysical.

What do we mean by metaphysical? Metaphysical means life beyond appearances, beyond life as we know it. What is the underlying thread that connects *all* of Life to ITself? One student was having trouble understanding the concept that there is only One Life, and we are all connected in some way. Upon waking one morning, she thought of a picture of cherries in cake batter. At first, she couldn't understand why she was thinking about cake, but then she got it. The answer to her question was a visual she could understand. (That's the beautiful way our inner being works with us—the spirit inside speaks to us in a language we can understand.) *We* are the cherries in the cake batter which connects us all.

If we take that a step further, imagine there is an invisible batter or substance that exists everywhere even though we can't see it. This substance gives life to all that is, whether it be a person or a rock. It is the very stuff of Life. This invisible substance not only connects us all together, IT sustains us. IT keeps us alive. Each one of us was created out of this life-giving substance in the form of our unique, individualized self. This Life is expansive and eternal. We are all living this One Life together. In physical form we express and experience life in our own special way, which gives us our own unique perspective on what is going on.

There is so much more to us than meets the eye. Here are some examples:

We think that we *are* our *bodies*.

Now, it's hard *not* to think we are our bodies because we feel our bodies and they are giving us messages all day long. We feel the pangs of hunger and thirst. We feel pain and pleasure from them. It's hard not to be focused on thinking that this is who we are. "I *am* the hunger, I *am* the pain, I *am* the discomfort." No, we are not the hunger, the pain or the discomfort. We are something more. We most definitely feel those things from time to time, but that doesn't mean that is who we are. The fact that we are not our bodies comes as a big surprise to many. Most of us believe that we *are* the whole package, whatever that is. The feedback we get from our bodies does *not* mean that is who we are. The diagnosis we get from a medical professional does *not* mean that is who we are. We are *not* the cancer. We are *not* our bodies.

If we are thinking we are our bodies (most people think this way because that idea is so ingrained in us and has never been replaced with a more accurate one), then it's easy to live in fear of losing our bodies. If we think this is all we are, we live in fear of *this* body aging, getting sick and dying. We live in fear of germs and illnesses that we might catch. When we begin to see any sign of deterioration, we start thinking we are going downhill and falling apart. If we don't have a better idea about our body, it will grow tired and old. If we have a greater idea of who we are and a vision of what is possible for our body, then it can serve us very beautifully, much longer than we ever expected.

Johann Wolfgang von Goethe was said to have "the body of a Greek god" when he passed away at the age of 83. There were no signs of aging. Because the outer world, which includes our bodies, reflects our inner thoughts, beliefs and emotions, his body was a testament to the kind of person he was and how he lived his life. Most of us have a long way to go with this idea, and yet it is always good to have a greater idea of what's possible to achieve.

Our bodies are designed perfectly. They are made of divine stuff and if given half a chance, they know how to heal and restore themselves to balance. They are hardwired to make sure they know how to do everything possible for our survival. They are here to serve the spiritual life within us. In order for that to happen, we have to be healthy. Disease is not natural, contrary to what the world says. We are not to focus on disease. It is not part of Life's design. Our bodies are a wonder of creation. They flourish when they are supported with a greater consciousness of health.

We think we *are* our *minds*.

We are *not* our minds. We are *not* our brains. We are *not* the thoughts we think. We are something so much more. We are the thinker or the observer *behind* the mind, watching it all. The mind is not controlling us. There is a thinker behind the mind that is in control. The thinker is our spirit. We are spirit, and spirit lives on forever. The mind and the body do not. It's up to our spirit to come through and get the mind and body working together on its behalf. Our body and mind are the vehicles through which our spirit moves about the world.

We think we *are* our *experiences*.

We are *not* the conditions we are experiencing. We are *not* our finances or the difficulties we may be having with others. We are *not* our gender, our sexual orientation, our socioeconomic status, the color of our skin, our past, our age, our mental health or any of the things we think describe us.

Michelangelo was writing love sonnets at the age of 89. He must have known he was something more. He didn't let his outer circumstances dictate what he could accomplish. There have always been people who have lived beyond their outer conditions or what the world thought possible. The only difference between them and the average person is that they continue to break through to even greater paradigms of what is possible by thinking expansive thoughts, thus raising the bar for us all. They keep on going. Thank God for those who lead the way and show us what is possible! It fuels our imaginations to create more.

I once approached a woman standing by the elevator as I left my hotel room, luggage in hand. We made small talk. I asked her what brought her to Pittsburgh? She said that she and her family were celebrating her grandmother's 106th birthday! Wow! That's not a number we hear every day. She asked why I was in Pittsburgh. She noticed I was all dressed up. I told her I was getting ready to give a talk at the Center for Spiritual Living. That opened the door for her to say a little bit more.

She said her grandmother is coherent, still gets around and keeps saying that she is ready to go home but she keeps on living. She gives all credit to God. I told her I was going to share that story. Why? It's not just because she has lived 106 years, but the fact that she is clear-minded and fully functional that makes her story is important to share. Even more, she recognizes her Source and gives credit where credit is due. Acknowledging a life backed by an Infinite Source... now that brings us closer to knowing that we are eternal beings!

Personal Journal Notes

_____

_____

_____

_____

_____

_____

_____

_____

_____

_____

_____

_____

_____

_____

_____

_____

_____

_____

_____

Concept 4: Spiritual Living

The definition of Spirituality: whatever it takes to keep your heart open.

~ Rev. John DePalma

Spirituality is a constant, consistent attempt to feel the Presence of God in everything and everyone.

~ Ernest Holmes

Spirituality is common goodness, human kindness, natural truth, brotherly love and heavenly worship. To be spiritual is to be normal.

~ Ernest Holmes

There comes a time when we feel that our small lives are not enough for us. We want more. We begin asking questions and actively seeking help. This conversation becomes foremost in our minds. Something inside of us knows there is more. Something deep inside of us is urging us to open ourselves up to a greater Unknown.

These are some of the things we may be experiencing:

- Things aren't working out for us, and the harder we try, the more frustrated we get.
- We are bored with what little we get from our lives and experiences, including our relationships. We lose interest and seek diversion.
- We believe that more exists than what we know.
- We believe that if we only knew more, we would be happy.

Anyone of these is reason enough for the search to begin so we can live a satisfying life. What kind of life would be more captivating and soul satisfying? When we open ourselves up to the greater Reality of Life, we begin to see that we have only been exposed to a very small portion of it. There's a much bigger game to play than the one we have been playing. We are ready to move into spiritual living.

What is spiritual living? Spiritual living is a deeper, more reflective, conscious and peaceful way of living. To live a spiritual life is to dedicate oneself to being a better person, one who comes up with more loving solutions. Spiritual living means supporting everyone and everything on the planet and all sentient beings. To live spiritually means to feel more life and love. Living this way helps people enjoy themselves because they are in touch with who they are as spiritual beings. Spiritual living creates individuals who are at peace with themselves. To be spiritual means to love, honor and respect ourselves. Living spiritually means to be happy with who we are. This way of life helps us to see ourselves as creators of productive, inspiring and fulfilling lives.

Living spiritually means creating a firm spiritual foundation from which to live and work. It is a proactive approach to life, and it means being present, having an awareness of what is possible and spending time focused on creating a better life for ourselves. It means being actively engaged with Spirit in everything. We don't have to wait for something bad to happen before we ask for help. Conscious or spiritual living means praying affirmatively, visualizing and visioning—especially when we feel we're on top of the world so that we keep our focus on what is right and good—and paying attention to the continuous impulses Life is already directing our way.

That includes seeing our self as divine, a higher order of being. Spiritual Living means to be respectful of all peoples, cultures, religions, traditions and countries whether we agree with them or not. It means appreciating the diversity of life, knowing we are all living the one Life together and that all roads lead home.

It means taking one hundred percent responsibility for our lives and what happens. Knowing how we see ourselves and others plays a part in the quality of our relationships. Seeing perfection helps to bring it forth. Seeing good everywhere we look brings forth more goodness, like Mother Teresa seeing the face of Jesus in everyone, including in the most distressing disguises.

It means genuinely caring for one another, willing to give whatever we have because we know our connection with an Infinite Source that is always providing more support, encouragement, upliftment, inspiration and love. Everyone needs to know that there is someone in their corner no matter what happens.

Spiritual living means taking ownership and responsibility for the care of Mother Earth, nature and our environment and treating it like it is our own. There is an Indian law that uses as a gauge for every decision how it will affect those to come seven generations from now. How mindful that is of preserving life for all!

It means living a life we can be proud of, thereby leaving a legacy for others to enjoy. Mentorship or being a good example of what is possible is incredibly valuable for those following in our footsteps. Why not stand on the shoulders of giants and gain an even greater perspective? We have the power to influence ourselves, our families and others right now in everything we say, think and do.

This way of living requires us to use our precious minds for constructive thinking about how to use our time, energy and love to create more of what we want to see.

Spiritual living means showing up to life every day, no matter what happened the day before, ready to give it our best. It takes great courage sometimes to show up to life, especially during difficult times. Each day we do, we stand tall in our truth and prove that we are greater than any experience we have.

Living this way puts the emphasis on peace, creating interesting, unique and innovative ways to live and share what we have with the world. When we work together globally, as one human family, we can enjoy the diversity, celebrating our unique and valid perspectives.

Becoming more spiritual opens us up to thinking ideas that have never been thought before, appreciating our precious minds, and even more, recognizing the thinker behind our thoughts that determines our existence...our true self. All of this opens us up to be a channel for Universal Wisdom.

Spiritual living sees every individual as a clear, open channel for good, a unique, individualized center of divine activity in the world.

Spiritual living helps us to appreciate our bodies, their intelligence, complexity, balance and health, how responsive they are to us, and how they support us as we move about the world. It means making decisions that hurt no one and embracing the highest good for all. We can never go wrong coming from a place of love. Life will support us fully as we consider what is best for all involved.

It means being dedicated to showing up with the highest, most loving, abundant consciousness possible. The greater our awareness and the bigger our perspective, the freer we become.

It also means participating in an ever-expanding and deepening relationship with the Infinite, whatever our definition or name we call IT. We yearn to come home to the innermost being within, that place where we connect with the Source of our being.

Living a spiritual life and reaping the benefits that bring us closer to God are the reasons we do our spiritual practices. Whatever they are to us, they are meaningful and keep us playing in the bigger game of Life.

This is a Journey that begins within--within me and within you. Let's take a look at how that works. Let's begin with... What is a practice?

Personal Journal Notes

_____

_____

_____

_____

_____

_____

Concept 5: A Practice

The highest reward for a person's toil is not what they get for it, but what they become by it.

~ John Ruskin

At the root of all habit is one basic thing: the desire to express life. There is an urge to express in all people, and this urge, operating through the channels of Creative Mind, looses energy into action and compels the individual to do something.

~ Ernest Holmes

Having a practice helps one to develop spiritually. What is a practice? We hear about athletes practicing and learning different maneuvers necessary for their sport. A practice is the habit of doing things in a certain way in order to achieve a desired result. It is something that we agree to do on a consistent and regular basis that will help us improve our performance. A spiritual practice is something that we do on a frequent basis that helps us develop spiritually in order that we may live a life with greater purpose and meaning. It helps us to bring a higher level of reverence to our lives versus going through the motions of doing only what is necessary to get by in life. Done effectively, it can leave us feeling more satisfied and fulfilled, which demonstrates as more happiness and success. A practice keeps us open and receptive to the Divine in the way of guidance, inspiration, confirmation and connection.

Sometimes we spend too much time figuring things out intellectually. Other times we lose our focus due to the number of distractions vying for our attention, leaving us feeling overwhelmed and worn out. In order to be more effective in how we live in this world, more is required. We need assistance. It's hard to manage all of our responsibilities with the complexity of today's world. We can't always do it alone, nor should we feel like we need to when there is divine wisdom, our intuition, that "still,

23

small voice within" speaking to us, urging us on. Inspiration can take us to a whole new place. It can give us a vision of something greater for ourselves, a new, evolutionary thought, a glimpse of a new possibility, or even shift the way we see things.

The idea of doing spiritual practices was totally foreign to me, even though I was brought up with formal prayers which we had to memorize. When I left the church during my teens, I didn't have any replacement for them, which left me out there on my own without any spiritual support.

I have always been attracted to psychology and self-improvement books. Wayne Dyer was one of my earliest finds, and I have enjoyed his work throughout the years.

Fresh out of college and desperately missing higher learning, I happened upon a highly elevated consciousness in *A Handbook to Higher Consciousness* by Ken Keyes. The concept of people living this way was inconceivable to me at that time. No one I knew came close to living like that. I couldn't believe it was even possible. After each decade of my life, I picked up that book again and looked at it. By my 40s, having studied New Thought, I began to see it was in the realm of possibility and that it would require a lifetime of practice to even come close to what Keyes was proposing.

In my early 30s, I was in dire need, and my coworker turned me on to *The Road Less Traveled* by Scott Peck. My whole life had just fallen apart, leaving me in a fragile state. This book gave me the insight to see that what I was really experiencing was a spiritual crisis, which led to everything else that happened. That was helpful to know. My embarrassed family told people I had a nervous breakdown.

From a young age, I was never a morning person, awaking happy and ready to go. Thankfully, that changed by my mid-30s when I started implementing a spiritual practice. At first, I did well to read a short prayer from *Creative Thought* magazine. While that may seem like a slow start, I soon noticed something different was happening. I liked feeling better, which led me to wanting to do more.

The practices described in this book build on one another but can also stand alone and be used separately. As mentioned earlier, I highly recommend reading through the entire book first. After that, you have the option of following the book and trying one exercise at a time or skipping to the one that speaks to you in that moment. Each of us knows what is best for our own needs. Spiritual living is not about following anyone else's rules or footsteps. Besides observing ancient wisdom teachings, our inner guidance directs us to what we need at any given time. This book is designed to be a resource to use as our inner self guides us.

In order to keep our lives and our practices juicy and inspiring, it is important that we change things up every now and then. It helps to keep them from getting routine. It's important to keep them alive. They were never meant to be drudgery, work or something we dread. Our spiritual practices are the fuel and spiritual nourishment we need to thrive every day. Like trying new recipes for food, we want to enjoy them and get everything we can out of our practices. We may even get some new ideas for a practice of our own.

A good friend and colleague, Dr. Kenn Gordon (Spiritual Leader for the Centers for Spiritual Living), said, "I spend two hours doing my spiritual practices every morning (praying, treating, reading, meditating) and the other 22 hours practicing what I learned." I have since read that the Dalai Lama spends five hours in meditation and spiritual practice each day. Most of us are in the thick of things, living in the world, and need even more spiritual support than someone living a more cloistered life. Interesting thought, isn't it? No one arrives at a point where they don't need to do them anymore.

Spiritual practices are an individual designation. We appoint them. We decide on which practices to commit ourselves. They may include a practice to stay in forgiveness, to live in gratitude and appreciation, to attend weekly services, tithe or stay present in the "Now" moment, to mention a few. Daily prayers, affirmations, setting intentions, visualization, visioning, mind treatments and anything else we decide to do may be a part of it. It could simply be spending time in nature, such as fishing or taking a nice walk.

Marriages, partnerships or other relationships can be a form of spiritual practice whereby one or both parties commit to bring their highest and best love and attention to their life together. A condition, a physical illness or facing a problem could be our spiritual practice if we decide to look at it that way and make it one. Even a hurricane can be a spiritual practice. Keeping oneself calm and centered in the middle of fears, worries and doubts requires a spiritual capacity not all of us have developed. Staying present and alert enough to follow our internal guidance system and direction requires strong spiritual muscles. How cool can we stay, not only for ourselves but for our families and those around us? There are plenty of natural disasters or storms that require us to keep our heads and be fully present so we can make the best decisions possible.

The Islamic faith is one of the fastest growing faiths in the world. Why? I believe one of the major reasons is the prayer rituals that are practiced at certain times throughout the day. Even though it may sound restrictive, it helps remind followers to check in with what is most important: God. People like to have guidance and direction. Five times a day they are required to stop what they are doing and pray... putting everything else aside while giving their undivided attention to praising God. It's easy to get off track in 24 hours, forgetting what really matters. This is a beautiful way to stay in alignment. We don't have to be Muslim to use this model and customize their practice to fit our own needs.

While that practice may not fit into our idea of a practice or even our schedule, implementing our own routine is of utmost importance. Maybe there are things that we require of ourselves like giving thanks before a meal, writing in a journal, reading something inspiring, walking in nature or writing thank-you notes. The more we incorporate practices throughout our days the more calm, cool and collected we can remain throughout. Daily rituals help us stay current with life so we can live from an elevated consciousness.

Whatever fills our cup and gets us in touch with joy is a personal way of taking care of ourselves spiritually. What follows are some of my favorite practices, along with their explanations. Each one has helped me in a different way with various parts of my journey. They all have helped me become who I am today.

Ready to get started?

Personal Journal Notes

_____

_____

_____

_____

_____

_____

_____

_____

_____

_____

_____

_____

_____

_____

_____

_____

_____

_____

Section II

Seven Ways to Exercise Our Spiritual Muscles

Part 1

Warmups/Detox/Reset/Basics/Ground Zero

The 1ˢᵗ Way: Move

We don't need more strength or more ability or greater opportunity. What we need is to use what we have.

~Basil S. Walsh

One who is a doer is magnetic and therefore infinitely more creative than any who merely hear. Be among the do-ers.

~ Neville Goddard

This is the place where it all begins: moving. Movement is the place to start if we want to use what we have and make it strong. Gently moving into these exercises increases our stamina, puts us in greater circulation and prepares our minds for what's to come. They also help us create new habits. Warm-ups' accomplish just that, getting our juices flowing and our body warmed up and limber so we can attain increased mobility. They will stretch us in ways we might not have expected or experienced before. They will also help get us started moving in the right direction.

Giving Thanks

Gratitude and appreciation are powerful exercises. Asking ourselves, "What am I thankful for today?" helps us to look for the good. We are well trained to see and judge what is wrong or what we don't like. I will never forget my teacher, Dr. Kennedy Shultz, saying if we had a big plastic garbage bag full of thank-you notes and letters saying wonderful things about us, and only one or two letters of complaint or criticism, we would be focused on the negative ones over all the others.

It's true, maybe there *is* something we need to look at in the one or two. Maybe there is nothing we can do about it. Obviously, we can't change the past. Is there something we can learn from them? Maybe it is more about the people who sent them than it really is about us. Of course, upon closer look, we need to pay attention to how much good we have generated. Most of us forget to focus on all the good, and there is always much more positive than negative. It's easy to criticize and complain. It takes effort to look at people and situations with love. When we do, we may be surprised to see all that is there.

There is something in the universe which forever gives ITself to ITs creation, forever offers ITself, not as a sacrifice, but as an impartation of ITs essence into everything.

~ Ernest Holmes

There is so much more going on than we are aware of in everything that happens. If we were conscious of all the possible mis-takes, we would see just how precious and pivotal each moment really is. There is an Intelligence operating perfectly throughout the world. None of us would be here today or have made it to this point in our lives if that were not true.

It is only as we come into union with good that we have the power of good. Evil[2] blocks itself, congests its own efforts, dams its own streams, and destroys its own purpose. Good cannot be blocked.

~ Ernest Holmes

If good is freely given and cannot be blocked, what is getting in the way of our enjoying more of it? The common denominator in all of our experiences can only be us. *We* are the ones who get in our own way. What can we do then, to open ourselves up to our greater good?

One of the most important things we can do is give thanks. All of the great spiritual masters recognized and taught the power of appreciation and the practice of giving thanks. Jesus said, "Father, I thank thee that thou hast heard me. And I know that thou hearest me always" (John 11:41-42).

---

[2]Evil, meaning a lack of good or love.

One year my husband and I started out for an early morning walk on Thanksgiving Day. I love walking, and it was even more important that day to do something extraordinary on this special day. Whenever we visit my brother Tom and sister-in-law Chris for Thanksgiving, our families go for a hike in the woods together that morning. However, we weren't together for this Thanksgiving. What could we do to make the day special? I was searching for more and a wonderful idea occurred to me.

At the start of our walk, I asked John what he was grateful for, and he said a few things and then was quiet. The idea came to me to take this up a huge notch. I jumped in, "Let me start by telling *you* what I am grateful for about *you!*" I proceeded to go on for 15 minutes or so about all of his qualities and aspects that I appreciate. I went places that I never had gone before. One thing led to another, and before we knew it, something magical had really taken place. He was excited to go next, and I got to hear things I never knew he thought or appreciated about me.

We went even further that morning and took each of our three grown children one by one, seeing them for who they really are. It was a heartwarming experience. The coveted Thanksgiving dinner couldn't stand up to what had just happened between us. This became our new Thanksgiving tradition for which I am extremely grateful! Now we make a point to share with our kids in person.

What more do we really need to say? It doesn't get any better than to see and experience God, Infinite Spirit, Life, continuously throughout our day, knowing that God always hears us and immediately responds to us. Just because we can't see this Presence and Power doesn't mean that IT's not there. We forget that IT is the one giving us the ideas in the first place. We need to prepare for the arrival of what it is we want. IT, The Thing ITself, God, is always working on our behalf. Giving thanks immediately puts us in right relationship with the Universe and opens us up to the greater flow of life and good. It is a prayer in and of itself.

Today, I am thankful for...

_____

_____

_____

_____

_____

We can also be grateful in advance for knowing we have something that hasn't quite demonstrated in our lives yet. This is part of the message, "pray believing." When we pray this way, with gratitude in our hearts, we are calling our desire into existence.

I am thankful in advance for...

_____

_____

_____

_____

_____

Regularly asking ourselves what we are grateful for and spending time each day in appreciation are the best ways to warm ourselves up and be in a good mood! Asking the Cosmic Intelligence, "How much better than this can it get?" is another great way to increase our expectation and capacity to receive gifts, signs, more good and more life that is waiting for us to move into position to receive.

Sharing Appreciation

Expressing our appreciation, complimenting and praising others, verbally or in writing, are beautiful ways to share our love and feelings. Sending thank-you notes to others is a great way to show appreciation for who they are and what they do. It's a deposit in theemotional bank account we share with others. It also helps them to appreciate themselves and what they do. Seeing people light up in response to our positive feedback or compliments on something remarkable they have done gives us all the energy we need to live more fully. It is a satisfying and rewarding act for us all.

Many times, it can even shift us from an undesirable mood and lift our spirits. Appreciating ourselves and others is a great warm-up exercise to get our juices flowing.

In what ways can I show greater appreciation to those around me?

_____

_____

_____

_____

Who do I need to appreciate more?

_____

_____

_____

_____

Journaling

Journaling is a wonderful exercise. We can start by just writing down observations about our day, or perhaps just the significant things that are happening in our lives that we don't want to forget. I have never wanted a tattoo, but there are people who use their bodies to document significant events in their lives, choosing art that represents certain milestones important enough to remember. Hopefully they won't run out of room once they up their game with more appreciation!

It doesn't matter that some of us aren't writers or didn't like writing while growing up or in school. We don't have to be good at it. This is a different kind of writing. There are no rules for expressing ourselves this way. We get to choose whatever it is we want to write, in whatever way we want to express it. Our expression can be through drawings or cut-out pictures from magazines. A good friend of mine cuts out words and pictures she likes each day. Picking from her collection, she creates sentences with ideas and words she would never have thought of on her own. These creations turn out to be powerful statements of Truth and Good. The process is divinely inspired, and often she is pleasantly surprised at how timely and perfect the message is. It's as if her higher self is speaking to her. That is the creative process in action at ITs best, a play between the human self and the Divine one.

I wasn't much of a writer because I never had much practice or instruction. I remember not having a clue where to start for the first talk I prepared as a minister. I could write a statement but then I froze. I had to discipline my mind to keep my train of thought long enough to communicate what wanted to be said. (It had been 15 years since I wrote college papers; I had forgotten how!)My husband taught me how to embellish my idea by connecting it to other sentences that would create a story. The more I did it, the better I got. It became a spiritual practice.

Our writing can be whatever we want it to be. It's for our eyes only. It's important that we don't judge what we write, or more importantly, ourselves. Everyone should have a place where we can talk to ourselves and write our thoughts, getting them down on paper and out of our heads. This helps us get a grip on what is going on and gets us out of an undesirable mental state.

The great genius, Leonardo da Vinci, was known to have journals filled with thoughts and ideas that came to him, sketches of plans and pictures he received. We don't have to be a genius to keep a composition notebook of things that are important to us. We might even have lists of things we want to do. We can reflect on each day and list the things we are grateful for.

Our journals can be whatever we want them to be. Life is a grand experiment and we are all spiritual adventurers and explorers. Incredible things happen every day in our lives that we may want to record and look back on. With the fast pace of today's living, it's often hard to remember all that transpired from one day to the next. Our days can be so chock full, we might even have a hard time remembering what happened earlier that day. From time to time it is good to review our prosperity and richness in life. Writing things down cements them in our consciousness and keeps our minds centered on things that make us feel good.

Keeping our attention on the goodness in our lives causes us to live in a state of appreciation, which is essential to attracting more. For the more difficult times, journaling can keep us on track, help us process our feelings and experiences, and help us look at them from a higher place so we can work from there.

Personal Journal Notes

_____

_____

_____

_____

_____

_____

_____

_____

_____

_____

_____

_____

_____

_____

The 2nd Way: Release

Your circumstances may be uncongenial, but they shall not long remain so if you perceive an ideal and strive to reach it. **You cannot travel within and stand still without** *[emphasis added].*
Divine Love is in control and all is well.

~ Catherine Ponder

But you, just as the vine is pruned by cutting away its useless branches and roots, prune your imagination by withdrawing your attention from all unlovely and destructive ideas and concentrating on the ideal you wish to attain.

~ Neville Goddard

Detoxing and fasts are great ways to clean out the body. Sometimes we experience symptoms that are not easy to explain, and this is a perfect way to reset the body and strengthen our immune system. Sometimes the body just needs to re-establish itself by cleaning out toxins and things we collect in the body, including all of our emotions stored there. Even flushing out the body with clean water can benefit our physical being immensely. Releasing is not only important for the body; it plays an essential role in our spirituality and makes room in us for greater living.

Creating an Opening/Clearing Space

Just as the body needs constant refueling and upkeep, so do our surroundings. Unnecessary, worn-out items easily clutter our space, distracting us from our focus and from doing the things we really want to do. This happens so gradually that we don't even notice the buildup; we've grown so accustomed to it. "Scope creep" is a business term used to describe having a contract to do a certain job, and then unexpected things that were not anticipated become part of the project as well. Suddenly we are doing more than we originally agreed to do, often without additional compensation. Scope creep happens in our homes and offices as well. It's hard to notice things that accumulate slowly over time and before we know it, our desks, shelves and closets are filled with things we really don't need and take up precious space. It's not until we realize what a clear, cleaned-out space could look like that we begin to see all that we have and begin to think about what could go.

Years ago, I visited a minimalist friend of mine. I loved the simplicity of his décor. His office was a clear space, free of unnecessary distractions. His books were on shelves in his closet. I remember thinking, *I could work in such a place.* Cleared and cleaned spaces help us to stay focused on the things that matter without being continuously distracted.

We are accustomed to being consumers, acquiring everything we think we could ever need or want. Most of us never learn how to release what we are done with or how to clean out regularly. I was fortunate to have a mother who always had a rotation going... a pile of things she was ready to release to Goodwill or one of the many non-profits that helps distribute used items to people in need. One of my high school teachers, a nun, said you only need three skirts. If you buy a new one, give one away. That may not work for everyone's lifestyle or profession, but it's a great idea to keep in mind. I never forgot that.

It's hard enough for us to get into the habit of purging. It's quite another to introduce our children to the idea. "Go clean your room" means nothing to a child. What does that even mean? Clean? I found that my son was very agreeable to letting things go because we had a policy in our house (which was small) that if he wanted to bring in more games and toys, he had to let some go.

Children outgrow their clothes so quickly. By trial and error my son and I learned best how to accomplish cleaning and clearing out by the following method: We would agree to concentrate on one section of the room for a short amount of time.

This shouldn't be a dreaded thing to do. No one wants to give up a day to do it all. This practice needs to become a part of our lifestyle. It can even be made into a game. I would raise an item, and he would say, "Yea,""Nay" or "Not sure." When he was preparing to move across the country for college, we did a major cleanout that made us both feel so good. This left him free to begin a whole new life.

By the time he was ready to leave, we were complete with our successful years together while he was growing up. We each gave it our best. It's not that we don't miss each other, but we know life is about growth, and it was time for each of us to branch out in new ways. Since he was moving across the country and would rarely be home, that last major cleanout opened a space for us to have a guest bedroom as well as a place for him to come home to.

Physical cleaning is therapeutic to the soul. It is essential for us to live a healthy, rich life. Most of all, cleaning and clearing frees up energy, which most of us say we want more of. Accumulating clutter and storing things take up energy and cause congestion within us and in our lives. It feels good to keep things in circulation, knowing others could be using what is no longer useful to us. Life is so much more than stuff; it wants to be lived by us in greater ways. Cleaning out can give us an instant lift and the feeling that we are making progress.

The activities above are external steps we can take. This workout prepares us for the more difficult internal exercises that are necessary for our growth and expansion. Cleaning our minds, our bodies and our external surroundings helps us to be ready for taking on more. Take time to make room for the new!

How can I create an opening in some area of my life?

_____

_____

_____

_____

_____

_____

_____

How can I clear space and rid my life of what no longer serves me?

_____

_____

_____

_____

_____

_____

_____

Forgiveness

When our son Joseph was 8, he had trouble sleeping. He had seen an advertisement on TV for a drug that could help people sleep. He pointed out that might be something that could help him. Today we hear that kind of thing all the time and don't give it much thought. This happened when those commercials were new, so a red flag went up in my mind, especially since it came it from a young one. I was disturbed first that my innocent child had been exposed to such nonsense during the early evening hours of family TV, and second, that he couldn't sleep. He often had issues sleeping, but it was evident that something deeper was going on. I decided to keep a closer eye on him.

After school a few days later while I was preparing dinner, he made a confession. He didn't always confess right away but when he did, we got it all. He has always been truthful and honest. Eventually he spilled the beans and told me everything. I could just see the relief he felt to be able to get this experience off his chest as he explained what happened. Telling someone we trust can really do that for us.

Here's what happened: His class was taking a test at school and Joseph happened to see some answers that he didn't have on the student's test next to him. He probably would have figured out the answers if he had just slowed down and thought about them. However, he felt nervous and glanced over at someone else's answers. At that moment he lost even more confidence in himself and wrote the three answers down. Then he thought about it some more and decided it didn't feel right.

As a qualifying question for decisions, we always asked him, "How does it make you feel?" or "How will it make your heart feel later?" Right then and there, he made the call to erase the answers and get them wrong instead. He was very proud of himself, and we were proud of him. His dad told him there are adults who would not have done what he did that day. His wholeness was revealed. His true self spoke to him. Seeing ourselves from a greater place and getting in touch with what is real and true is the most important thing and will answer our questions and concerns, including helping us sleep peacefully!

Forgivingness is key. It's interesting when we separate the word, *for-give-ness*, or substitute *for-giving-ness*. *For* is the reason why. *Giving* is for giving something. It's for giving something to ourselves. It's for giving something to the other person. While it's important to give to another person, our forgiveness is most important to *us*. We're the ones that get the real benefit. We don't know whether someone else will accept our forgiveness or possibly reject us. It's important for us to do it, mostly for ourselves because it frees us up from being blocked. It's not always easy when we're in the heat of the moment and there's something that has happened that has hurt us deeply or hit us personally. However, as quickly as we can explore whatever that feeling is and turn it around, the faster we feel relief.

How much time do we spend looking at our past? How much more time do we spend on what once was, or what is currently happening versus planning for something better to happen in our future?

If we think back on our mistakes, or the crazy things we did, or problems we created, or people we hurt, we may want to dig a hole and bury ourselves in it. That doesn't do us or anyone else any good. There are gems to be mined out of those experiences, things we learned that can become our most precious possessions if we see them properly. Knowing these things, we can keep on going, creating from a more loving and evolved place moving forward.

Yes, there might be some clean-up to do. There might be some damage control...what we could call *aftermath*. The most important thing is that we get on with the business of living and creating more of what we *do* want to see and experience.

Forgiveness is the fastest way for us to get out of our entanglements. It keeps us from holding onto any unfinished business that drains our energy and keeps us from living fully in our present moment where we could be creating something new and wonderful for all.

We don't stand a chance for happiness when we hold grudges or resentments or refuse to forgive. Those behaviors put us out of alignment with our true, divine nature and when we do them, the result is that we get more of the same. It comes back to us. When we forgive, we set ourselves free and move back into alignment with our nature. When we do this, we put ourselves in the flow of everything good. We are held to a richer existence because of who we are. We know when we are out of alignment with our free self. We can feel it. We know when we are in alignment with our inner self because it feels fabulous when we are. Forgiveness is a tool that can help us get back on track.

When we practice forgiveness, letting go of the lesser and making room for the greater, we prepare for our own resurrection from any undesirable or unfavorable conditions by cleansing and clearing our own stuff. In that place we have the energy, courage and love to begin again and move into the unknown with confidence and trust, knowing our future can only be brighter and better.

Forgiveness is an excellent warm-up exercise because it gets things moving that have been stuck and puts us in right relationship with ourselves and the Universe. There is circulation where there was once blocked energy. Only we can do that for ourselves, and ultimately it will make us more agile in our spiritual development.

Here's a place to begin:

I am willing to forgive_____ for

_____

_____

_____

_____

I forgive myself for _____

_____

_____

_____

_____

I forgive _____ for

_____

_____

_____

_____

Don't look back. Prepare to move ahead! It's the only way. Forgiveness is important for exercising our spiritual muscles and building our spiritual strength. It does wonders for our self-esteem and gives us peace of mind and heart.

How could my life be freer and easier if I forgave this person, this situation, or myself?

_____

_____

_____

_____

_____

Ho'oponopono

How we see ourselves and others makes a difference in the quality of our lives. More than likely, at any given time there will be someone or something someone does that gets under our skin. It matters not how big or small. It is not enough to say that is the nature of being human and living with others. As spiritual beings, we have to find a way to make peace with ourselves and those around us. The *Ho'oponopono* prayer is a way in which we can get back to a state of balance and harmony.

Ho'oponopono is a sacred Hawaiian healing prayer, specifically used by Dr. Hew Len, a psychiatrist who borrowed the practice from the local tradition of their spiritual leaders. He headed a psychiatric wing of a hospital in Hawaii. His use of this prayer was so effective that they eventually shut down this wing because everyone was healthy enough to be released. *Zero Limits,* by Joe Vitale, is an entire book focused on the process.

For those of us who are not familiar with the Ho'oponpono prayer, it goes like this:

> *I love you.*
> *Please forgive me.*
> *I am sorry. (I am sorry for seeing you this way.)*
> *Thank you.*

The word itself is a powerful prayer that can be used as a mantra. Repeating the word, *Ho'oponopono* again and again is an effective way to release negative charges in us regarding ourselves and/or others.

Years ago, our family was vacationing in Vero Beach, Florida. Friends had allowed us to use their house, which was only a block away from the beach. My son Nick and I were so excited about this spiritual exercise that we couldn't wait to get started. By repeating the steps to the prayer over and over again, as we walked along the beach, we washed and cleansed every uncomfortable, disturbing memory we could think of from our past. There wasn't a stone left unturned. We wanted to take care of it all. It was a very healing time for us both and freed us up immensely.

When circumstances arise where we need to forgive ourselves, we can use the prayer this way:

> *I love you.*
> *Please forgive me.*
> *I am sorry. (I am sorry for seeing you [myself] this way.)*
> *Thank you.*

This exercise came in handy when I had what some might call an anxiety attack while I was trapped by myself in a friend's desolate mountain home for days because of the snow. I knew that I was creating more trouble for myself because I couldn't stop my fearful thoughts. I was immersed in fear and faced deep-seated things I hadn't dealt with before. I knew my thoughts had grown more powerful through my practices, which meant I could more easily attract experiences that matched my fears. Knowing I was actively creating a negative experience only intensified my fears. Somehow, I needed to neutralize my thinking and bring myself back to a state of peace and harmony. In my moment of panic, my wonderful son Nick called. He just happened to want to share an experience he just had in his own life using the *Ho'oponopono* prayer.

I knew in that moment that I had been heard. Infinite Intelligence had acted through my son's phone call at the exact moment of my need. Nick is not a caller. I don't hear from him often, but when I do, you can bet it is going to be something that benefits us both greatly. I knew I was on top of this mountain by myself and even though I could see neighbors' houses at a distance all around me, I felt very much alone. To my surprise, some old victim consciousness had surfaced. To receive his call in the quiet of the dark, wintery evening was like getting a call from God, ITself. I smiled. What was his message?

As soon as we ended our call, I went to work. As I repeated those words, *I love myself. I forgive myself. I am sorry to see myself this way. Thank you ...* again and again. As I did, my breathing eased. I felt the anxiety diminish. I imagined a fountain of love coming up from within me, washing away everything unlike itself.

I had thought my purpose in the mountains was to write my book, but Life seemed to have a different, more important agenda for me. I felt frustrated that things didn't seem to be going my way. It wasn't until the end of my trip, with the help of my prayer treatment partner and good friend, Sam, that I realized the real work I was there to do was to work on myself. Caught up in the middle of it, I hadn't realized what was going on. The real purpose of my being there was to face myself, to look at what I had previously glossed over in my own life: situations that happened in my past which I didn't know how to handle and had buried. Three different situations occurred during my most vulnerable time after leaving my first husband. All of them involved unwise choices I'd made from my victim mindset that had put me in danger. This retreat time away created an opening for them to come to the surface. My real purpose was to embrace those areas in me that I had neglected. *I* was being worked with. I got to clean up some of my old stuff so I could get to know my inner self better. That really needed to happen before I could finish writing so that I could really touch my readers in a more meaningful way and help turn on a light bulb for them as well as for myself. I had set an intention to do something good, and the Universe made it into something even more wonderful! The full intention played out for everyone's good. The story I ended up getting was so much better than anything I had imagined.

A few years ago, my son Nick and I each had a car accident within 24 hours of each other, and though both of our cars were totaled, neither of us were severely harmed. He was in Oregon, on the other side of the country from Florida. The good news was that we had been barely touched, and cars can be replaced. It did give me pause to think how much responsibility we have for our thoughts, to think that they can affect those close to us to some degree or another, even across the country from each other. I know that my children have responsibility for their own thoughts as well, and I am not totally responsible for theirs. Even so, I had to ask myself, *What part did I play?* Obviously, I had some things going on that had put me in that position. Whatever it was at the time, I had to love and forgive myself. This was another opportunity to use the *Ho'oponopono* prayer.

We don't necessarily use tools or exercises like this all the time, but when something triggers, going to a simple prayer like this can bring our salvation. If someone cuts us off in traffic, or we take something offensively, or feel misunderstood, or someone vents in front of us, we have an immediate way to deal with our feelings. *I love you, please forgive me for seeing you like this.* These are the kinds of words we want to have readily available that will help turn things around on the spot. Interactions with people and the world can bring up things rather suddenly. We can take better and quicker care of ourselves if we can move on these things as soon as possible. We want to have tools in our spiritual toolbox that we can pull out at a moment's notice. The more quickly we take care of things as they happen, the easier it is for everyone in the long run.

The *Ho'oponopono* prayer allows us to rectify an error. We merely say those four simple lines: *I love you; Please forgive me; I'm sorry; Thank you.* Those four wonderful lines do the trick. Whenever something comes up that we need to forgive, this prayer is a way of cleaning or clearing our mind of whatever is toxic that has been ignited, or of a memory that has been triggered. Sometimes we don't even know why we feel bad or what we feel bad about. We don't even know why we feel bad from one moment to the next. We had been feeling good, and then suddenly we are in the middle of experiencing a memory. The *Ho'oponopono* prayer is a way of washing those disturbing or upsetting memories. Love flows through our mind and rids us of unwanted thoughts. It takes the sting out of the bite. It makes distasteful thoughts more palatable than before. It helps us get through them to the other side where we can once again see with eyes of love, as God sees, from a loving point of view.

We can use this as a mantra and see how magnificently its healing quality makes us feel and works in whatever situation we find ourselves, where we need more help. This is an exercise we can use to build our spiritual muscles and keep ourselves fit

I love _____.
Please forgive me for seeing you this way,
I am sorry.
Thank you.

Advanced Journal Exercise: Morning Pages

When things are particularly difficult, I recommend doing the Morning Pages. I discovered this beneficial technique years ago while leading a book discussion group at a local bookstore. More information can be found about it in *The Artist's Way* by Julie Cameron. For those who are emotionally upset or traumatized, this is a good way to start working through things on their own, guaranteed to break up icebergs (blocks), and cool down volcanoes. When we don't know what to do and can't get out of our current state of mind and heart, this is just the thing.

Every morning we put pen to paper and start writing whatever we are feeling. We can swear, yell, scream, and say whatever we want to say on paper to someone else, to ourselves, to God. Don't worry--God, Source, won't care. It is healthy when we give ourselves permission to let it all out. Some people scream into pillows, but generally, this is much more effective. This writing is *not* done to be shared with others. In fact, this work is for our eyes only. I wouldn't put this stuff in my journal for someone to find after I am gone. Some of these outpourings in my past were so lethal that I didn't have the stomach to read them ever again. I wrote them on a separate piece of paper so that I could tear them up or burn them soon afterward. No one, especially our loved ones, needs to be exposed to such wrath. As horrible as this sounds, these writings gave me back my sanity. There are some things that can't be shared, and we need a way to handle them ourselves. Peace of mind ruled the day again! An opening was created for good feelings and ideas to come through. I was more myself than ever. When I got to that place, I no longer needed to read those writings again.

The Morning Pages exercise is for getting rid of toxic thoughts and emotions in our minds and bodies. Getting those things out leaves us feeling refreshed and renewed. The instructions say to write three pages each morning, day after day, until welcome to a point where we are completely out of bad things to say and find ourselves in a new place. Artists use this process to create an opening for the flow of creativity. I highly recommend it for any kind of processing that needs to be handled privately.

What am I holding onto or carrying with me that is getting in the way of my moving forward?

_____
_____
_____
_____
_____

How could I use Morning Pages to help me release my negative emotions?

_____
_____
_____
_____
_____

Personal Journal Notes

_____

_____

_____

_____

_____

_____

_____

_____

_____

_____

_____

_____

_____

_____

_____

_____

_____

The 3rd Way: Listen

'You cannot command me so greatly that I cannot work by you still more greatly,' is the constant whisper of our Secret Self.

~ Emma Curtis Hopkins

We spend a good amount of time exerting energy and expressing outwardly. The methods described below will help us develop more passive ways of being in the world. Receiving is every bit as important as giving. When we put ourselves in a receptive mode, we create an opening for information we might otherwise miss. Receiving opens us up to the full experience of life. Below are some ways we can exercise our minds and bodies so that we become adept at reading what's going on within and around us.

Breathe

We may remember from grade school science lessons that the oxygen we breathe is a byproduct of photosynthesis, which is the process whereby plants take in sunlight to synthesize food from carbon dioxide and water. The plants receive from us our waste--what we can't use anymore--and make something wonderful: oxygen for us all, humankind and animals alike. In addition to the very breath we need to survive, plants give us an amazing source of food, as the plant itself.

The oxygen released by plants is vital to respiration for people and animals. The carbon dioxide we release is vital to plants. The process of photosynthesis is therefore considered the ultimate source of life for all here on Mother Earth. We couldn't live without it! It is the key to life!

This interchange is going on continuously whether we are aware of it or not. We are involved in an ongoing cycle of giving and receiving...giving to life with our breath and receiving from life with each new breath we take.

Just like breathing, Life is a circular pattern, a circle in every area...in the area of energy, love and divine substance as money or good...whatever goes out, must come back. It is a universal law.

Behind it all is Source, the Creator of all, which doesn't just give us a part of Itself, IT gives *all* of ITself, as much as we can receive, in the form of air or anything else.

I can't count the number of times my husband has told our son, "Just breathe!" Whenever Joseph was upset, John would tell him, "Take some breaths. Take a few big, deep breaths before you say anything." I was trained right along with him, and I can't tell you how handy it has been when faced with something overwhelming. Just hearing those words can be a wonderful reminder that everything else can wait...a pause button can be pushed. Facing unexpected news, which is often difficult, requires that we get ourselves in order first before we can get to the place of "everything's going to be okay."

We have a choice to either react to the madness (or temporary insanity) immediately or to approach it from a more composed place. Breathing is something simple and easy we can do at once to help ourselves feel better.

How can we think straight when we feel like we are going to explode or ready to pop like a balloon? Nothing good can come from that place of extreme pressure. Focusing on our breathing allows us to relieve some of the pressure. So often we say things in the heat of the moment that we don't really mean because we don't take a moment to collect ourselves and come from a higher, more loving place. Once the words are out there, we can't bring them back and end up regretting them after hearing the whole story.

I observed my daughter, Liz, working in this way with her twin daughters, Aubrey and Everly, when they were as young as 8 months. Twins are an especially sensitive dynamic. They must learn patience early on, while they take turns having their needs met. Moms can only do so much. When either of them would start to get upset, Liz would softly remind them, "Take a breath. Breathe in. Breathe out." She would breathe right along with them. It was amazing to watch and see how effective this technique really was. I am sure it helped Liz keep calm as well.

Breathing is an excellent way to blow off some steam and pull ourselves together. Using an interruption strategy such as taking a breath instead of an immediate response of frustration is a perfect spiritual exercise and builds our spiritual muscles. There are plenty of opportunities in this world to restrain ourselves from saying things we shouldn't and from doing things we have no business doing. This requires discipline and takes practice. Practice makes perfect.

I remember to breathe whenever this person, problem, or situation comes before me:

_____

_____

_____

_____

Silence

Can we be still? What does that mean? How comfortable are we with no TV or music playing? No news? No radio playing in the car? Being all alone with ourselves, giving ourselves a break from the noise with silence? Do we have to have something on every waking moment? If so, what is that all about? Is it a habit or a need?

Some people need to have some noise while they are sleeping. I was shocked while staying with a friend and her family years ago. Music played all night throughout the house from a radio in the parents' bedroom. For them and their children, it was the most natural thing in the world. For me, who was used to absolute silence, it most definitely didn't work. I laid awake on their couch all night long. Thank God, I was only there for one night!

Being still and sitting in silence is a perfect way to get into alignment with the natural rhythm of our bodies, giving them time to regenerate without interference. It also gives us a chance to hear ourselves think and to pay attention to the still, small voice within that speaks to us.

It may be a shock for some to go cold turkey with this practice of being in silence. Working our way into more silence can be done in small increments. We may be surprised how relaxing it is and the calming effect silence can have on us as we get used to it. Building this muscle is key to our spiritual strength and being able to receive the input necessary for living a more intentional life.

Am I able to be still?

_____

_____

_____

_____

How comfortable am I with being alone?

_____

_____

_____

Can I begin to appreciate a few minutes of quiet time and give myself the gift of being refreshed?

_____

_____

_____

_____

_____

Advanced: Day of Silence

"I am declaring today a Day of Silence, "one of my good friends announced as she came out to the kitchen where her partner was cooking. They lived in the same house, worked mostly from home, and had ample time together. In fact, maybe a little too much. One day she decided she needed a Day of Silence, which meant she needed peace and quiet and asked to be supported in this way by her partner. This meant that the partner would automatically be included in the Day of Silence, too!

I remember how impressed I was to even hear of such a thing. I had never thought of making such a bold request, much less expect to get a day being left alone in my own home with loved ones around. I haven't had to pull that card yet, but I am keeping it in my back pocket for when I do. Just because we don't live in a monastery doesn't mean there aren't times when we really need to just *be*—to be quiet, listen, enjoy silence and rest. There is something so healing and restorative about being quiet. Sometimes we are not in a good place, more than likely with ourselves. Whatever it is, having a moratorium on our conversations and activities can be just the thing we need to come back to a place of love, harmony and balance. It may be the most loving thing we can do for *all* involved.

How long can I go without talking?

_____

However long I maintained silence, how did I feel?

_____
_____
_____
_____

Be Present

Are we present and listening with our full attention to those with whom we are speaking (especially family members) and not thinking about other things or what we want to say next? Are we present to each other? Are we asking each other about our day? Listening to what is being shared? Taking a genuine interest in those we are close to? Are we having dinner together and really being present with one another, or are we in our own world of smart phones? Is it still possible to ask our husbands, wives, partners and children to come together at a specified time each day? So many unexpected surprises are waiting to emerge when we create time together, sharing beautiful, healthy foods and rich conversations over the dinner table. Yes, it does take extra effort and perhaps putting up with some initial resistance to make this kind of requirement of our family members. It also helps us develop our emotional intelligence and communication skills, both essential for relationship development. No man is an island. We need each other. The rewards that come from living with greater purpose are irreplaceable, and the memories of those precious times stay with us forever.

Can I be present to those around me?

_____

_____

Can I be present to my loved ones?

_____

_____

Can I be present to myself and my own needs?

_____

_____

Live in the Now

We get so busy planning or worrying about our to-do lists and everything that needs to be done that we often find our minds drifting somewhere else and not fully engaged and living in the present moment. The moment we have right now is the only moment we really have. What has gone before is history. There is little we can do about it. What is in our future is what we can do something about. It may not play out anything like we thought it would, but we do have some say in how we think and respond to whatever is going on. It is imperative while we plan and create our next steps for the life we desire that we stay open and present to all the gifts that are happening around us in this very moment.

Staying present to the *now* moment, and the next *now* moment, is the connection point to all the Power and Intelligence that is always available to us. When we are in this place of being totally focused, fully connected and putting all of our energy into the present, we are magnificently open to the flow. There is a reason why *now* is so important.

I also love the practice of asking myself, "In this moment, do I have everything I need?" The answer is always *yes*. In this now moment, I have everything I need, at least for the moment. Asking again in the next moment, "Do I have everything I need *now*?" Once again, the answer is yes. In both the moment that just passed and the one I am currently in I have everything I need. This is a great exercise in training us to see how much we already have and how well we are always taken care of. Why would I ever think I wouldn't have what I need when every time I check, I do? This exercise helps us to stay in the moment and appreciate feeling that right now my immediate needs are being met, as they always have been and always will be, forever and ever. Knowing that, we can relax and be ourselves.

What does it mean to me to live in the Now?

_____
_____
_____
_____

How does it feel to live in the Now?

_____
_____
_____
_____

How does it feel when I am fully focused on what is before me?

_____
_____
_____
_____

How does it feel to give my total attention to the Now moment versus giving attention to the past or future?

_____
_____
_____
_____

Contemplation

When asked what her preferred spiritual practice was, a colleague responded: contemplation. I had never heard of that as a specific practice before. We often don't view just thinking about something as a form of spiritual practice because there is hardly a moment when we aren't thinking. We may discount our negative thoughts as unproductive and often destructive, but even negative thoughts and processing can lead us where we want to go. Allowing ourselves to sit with things in a calm and peaceful manner often leads us to a place of greater realization. Yes, contemplation is a useful spiritual exercise to practice, especially when we are conscious of and in control of where our minds are taking us.

Opening ourselves to receive new thoughts and ideas is a practice in itself. It means having a keen awareness of what is going on, being able to connect the dots (make associations, put ideas together) and listen to the Spirit within us speak and guide us. When we are open to the idea that something greater is going on than we can put our finger on, Spirit will help us get the fullest interpretation of what is happening to the degree that we are capable of understanding and appreciating. Life will take us as far as IT can with where we are, and when we are ready for more, IT will take us further.

Do I allow myself time to sit and think?

_____

_____

_____

_____

What benefits do I receive from contemplating my life?

1. _____

_____

2. _____

_____

3. _____

_____

4. _____
   _____
5. _____

Meditation

The purpose of meditation is to recognize that you are already free. In the deepest part of you nothing has ever happened.

~ Andrew Cohen

Enough can't be said about the power and benefits of meditation as a regular exercise to build our spiritual strength. Just taking 20 minutes twice a day not only releases tension, it also leaves us with a new state of mind from which to work, greater awareness and more peace. Our decision to allow more ease in our lives in every possible way is key to living successfully in today's world. With all the components of stress, strain and pressure it's easy to see why inflammation is considered the number one cause of our physical problems. It's also plain to see why an inflamed consciousness would lead to outbursts of anger, hatred and fear. Those are the logical outcomes of intense, out-of-control living. The good news is that we get to decide the kind of life we live, or at least for now decide how we are choosing to live with the conditions that make up our life.

There is a part of us that is unaffected by anything we have ever experienced. When we meditate, we have access to that place where nothing has ever happened and everything and anything is possible. It truly is a powerful exercise—one of the most valuable spiritual fitness exercises we can do that will result in a multitude of benefits for us to enjoy.

One of the most inspirational books I have read is Immaculee Ilibagiza's life story, *Left to Tell: Discovering God Amidst the Rwandan Holocaust.* Immaculee lived for days on end hidden in a bathroom with a group of women. There was no room to move. They were barely fed. Everyday they were spared a brutal death. One day she realized that she must be being saved for something special to do; otherwise, why would her life continue to be spared when her people were being slaughtered all around them?

What a revelation! She was able to have such an epiphany in the middle of one of the most horrible times and under some of the worst conditions that humans can endure because she stayed in the practice of prayer and meditation for most of her waking hours (approximately 15-20 hours a day). It's not easy to sleep crouched on the floor next to others, so she did the only thing she could: pray. What else could she do? She communed with the Infinite right where she was, receiving information she would otherwise not have gotten.

She prayed to know the reason she continued to be given the gift of life. Each day she thanked God for being alive another day, even though they experienced one difficulty after another. One day she heard the minister who was hiding them say that the U.N. decided to send troops. A light bulb came on for her. In that moment, she knew the Rebel Tutsi Army would win; that she and others would talk with English-speaking people, telling them all that happened. She had a premonition that she would work with the U.N. She knew right there and then that she must learn how to speak English.

She asked God what she needed to do. Then she asked the minister if she could use his French/English dictionary and any other books he might have in English (French was their second-ary language at the time). Having practiced being quiet for so long, she had developed the art of listening and paying attention, accessing the Divine Mind, which knows all. Because of her sharpened awareness she picked up on subtleties and received information that she otherwise would not have been privy to. She received guidance regarding the preparation she would need to be ready when the time came.

Doing her spiritual practices and following her intuition put her in alignment with the greater Intelligence that knows all. She was then ready and willing to play a much bigger part in the situation. Eventually, after they found a way out, she got a job working for the U.N. and was able to help many more people. That kind of courage can only come from aligning oneself with a higher Power and following IT's lead.

Andrew Cohen, author of *Evolutionary Enlightenment,* wrote that we must meditate as if our life depends on it. In actuality, it does. This is what Immaculee did for her every waking hour, and every detail played out to the tee in support of freedom for her and those who were with her.

Those are the kinds of things that can happen when we prepare ourselves to be a vehicle through which Spirit, Infinite Intelligence, God, can work. It can open doors for us which lead to a whole new life.

Meditation is a beneficial spiritual tool because it opens us, and the more we can breathe our body into that relaxed and peaceful state, the easier it becomes to detach from everything going on around us. It takes us back to a new set point. It's a blissful timeout we give ourselves...a chance for refreshment and renewal. Even though we may feel like nothing is happening, the more we meditate, the more we notice little things that we wouldn't have before, and unexpected things happen. New beginnings are possible from this enlightened state.

One year my husband was watching the Super Bowl. I was in and out of the kitchen, making various things to eat. I can't sit still for a whole game. I was happy with cooking and coming back to see how things were going. I had heard somewhere that the Seattle Seahawks (one of the teams playing) used meditation and yoga as part of their regular practice. That piqued my curiosity. I was anxious to see who would win. I wanted to know if it really gave them an edge. Obviously, this was a spectacular team to be in a Super Bowl game. The question for me was, "What is it that makes one team win over the other, especially when they have been neck-and-neck the whole game?"

In this case they didn't win, but I happened to catch a play at the end as I walked into the room. The ball was thrown to one of the Seahawk players who couldn't quite grasp it, but the very motion of the ball tumbling through his fingers was taking him yards farther down the field, closer to the goal. Finally, he caught it! That play (which seemed very unlikely to ever happen in the first place) and the yardage it gained his team were amazing!

That is exactly the kind of thing that happens when we meditate. The unexpected, or unusual, happens in our favor.

Something changes suddenly that somehow takes us further along. It could be the answer or solution to something we couldn't figure out. It could be that we meet someone who has the answers or next steps for us. It's nothing we can plan or predict. We can't even prepare for it. We just keep up the practice, and it comes in from left field.

In the case of the football player, there are not enough physical workouts a player could do to make that sort of thing happen. We couldn't plan for something like that to happen, no matter how hard we try. Little things happen which we wouldn't necessarily pick up on that brighten our day and help us to see that we are working with more than just our small personality selves and the physical world. We notice that things start going our way more often. Some might call it *grace*. Once we have experienced it, we say, "Yes, I want more of that!" This is the kind of life I want to be living. It's the kind of life we were all created to live.

It's been reported that we think 60,000 or more thoughts per day. They happen so quickly that there is no space in between for inspiration or to hear spirit speak to us. We are continually taking in and putting out thoughts, analyzing, unless we make room for something greater to come in. If we think of every thought as a bubble, then the spaces between the bubbles, or thoughts, is where enlightenment or inspiration can come. Could we all enjoy more understanding, upliftment and vision? I believe we can.

Meditating can be as easy as sitting still for a few minutes and focusing on our breathing. As we become more comfortable with the amount of time we have set aside, we can stretch our meditating muscles by increasing the amount of time. We may even find ourselves not wanting to leave such a blissful state. Listening to a guided meditation can also bring us back to center and give us composure to work with throughout our day. For example, Deepak Chopra and Oprah Winfrey have wonderful guided meditations which include a focus for the day and about 10 minutes of quietly reciting a Sanskrit mantra. Mantras help us stay in a meditation by giving our minds something to do while we just *be*. Using Sanskrit mantras gives us the added benefit of repeating their healing words, letting them soak in and allowing them to become a part of us.

Am I willing to take a few minutes for myself each day to sit still and listen?

_____

_____

_____

_____

_____

How does meditation enhance my life?

_____

_____

_____

_____

If I already meditate, how can I increase the time or quality of the time I spend this way?

_____

_____

_____

_____

_____

Walking Meditation

Walking meditation is one of my favorites. It is great for those who are used to being active. It keeps our bodies moving and frees up our minds for higher thoughts.

One day our son and daughter, Nick and Liz, were talking about what happened on their walks during one of their visits. We have a lovely wooded walkway we can take through our neighborhood and the next. One day we compared notes and learned that unknowingly, we were each having the same kind of experience. It didn't matter whether we were walking alone or together. We didn't plan for it to be that way, it just was.

For the first mile or so we let our minds wander and thought about whatever we wanted to think about. As we acclimated to the great outdoors and headed back toward home, we each made a conscious decision to think only good thoughts, or to consider what changes we needed to make regarding things with which we were currently involved.

It was almost as if nature itself was directing our walks. Going out, our minds were not always in the right place, or they were nowhere in particular at all. Along the way, with nature all around us and filling us up with its amazing energy, we were channeling a higher vibration, which made us think more loving, abundant and productive thoughts. (Endorphins were also being released in our bodies because of our physical activity.)

Walking and being in nature is one of the best things we can do for our health and well-being. When we can't do anything else, we can walk. If we can't walk, we could just step out into nature for a few minutes at a time. We can look at the expansiveness of the sky and get in touch with something greater. It's a wonderful adventure when we let nature have its way with us. We can put ourselves in nature and just *be*, letting life lift our spirits and seeing how quickly everything changes. Our bodies will appreciate moving about as well, by our stretching them and making them more flexible. Walking meditation is great exercise for the spirit, mind and body.

How can I increase my time in nature?

_____

_____

_____

_____

_____

What are some places I could walk and be surrounded by natural beauty?

_____

_____

_____

_____

_____

How would spending time in those places make me feel?

_____

_____

_____

_____

_____

Exercise Rituals

Walking, running and swimming are some of the best ways to exercise the body and free up the mind to do affirmations, mantras or rituals we make up. I love having little rituals built into my day that help me stay on track. One is saying good morning to God, good morning to the world. It's a simple thing but it gets me started on the right track for my day early on. Rituals can be incorporated into our physical exercise as long as we are safe in doing them and able to benefit from both.

An example would be focusing on the aspects of God:
TRUTH, LIFE, LOVE, SUBSTANCE, INTELLIGENCE
Omniscient, Omnipotent, Omnipresent
All Knowing, All Powerful, Everywhere equally present.
We can do this while walking, running or swimming... maybe even while doing the dishes.

Next, I may take one of the qualities and focus entirely on that:
TRUTH
Omniscient, Omnipotent, Omnipresent
All Knowing, All Powerful, Everywhere equally present.
Then another:
LIFE...
On and on for as long as we want to go.

I use it as a mind wash. It keeps my mind clean and focused on the most ideal thoughts. We could even use a prayer in this scenario. Whatever we come up with is something that brings us joy and is personal to us. That way it benefits us the most.

The ancient practice of yoga is also an excellent way to achieve amazing results as we connect our mind, body and spirit.

What are some exercise rituals I could do?

1. _____
   _____

2. _____
   _____

3. _____
   _____

4. _____
   _____

If I am already doing some rituals of my own, how can I vary what I am doing to keep things fresh and new for me?

1. _____
   _____

2. _____
   _____

3. _____
   _____

Nighttime Questions

Before bedtime is the perfect time to ask a question of our higher self or subconscious mind that is busy working 24/7. While we are asleep and out of the way, our mind can more easily focus on giving us an answer. It may come in the form of a dream, clarity or a specific idea. The answer might be right there when we wake up or it may take longer, depending on how ready we are to receive the answer. Our answer could be dependent on an action step we feel called to take. If so, it is important that we take that step and follow the "yellow brick road" to see where it leads.

We may think we are ready for the answer, and yet maybe we aren't. Everything comes to us in divine right and perfect timing. If we are asking, it means our awareness is there and we are beginning to pay attention. We are in the ballpark of being receptive.

Even if we don't get the answer to the question we are asking before we retire for the day, we may be receiving information that will lead us to it. There may be steps for us to take, and it's up to us to follow through. The Universe is rich with information. IT is always operating on our behalf, whether we know it or not, and preparing us for the fulfillment of our desires if only we will get out of the way and allow it.

Too often we come up with reasons we can't do or have a certain thing. The Universe can only say, *Yes! Yes, you can! Yes, you can go to Paris...* or *Yes, you can't go,* depending on the call we, ourselves, make. We may be the ones talking ourselves out of the chance to go to Europe or whatever else we want that is on the table. The Universe has the ways and means to make it all happen. We are the ones that put on the brakes by coming up with excuses why things can't be. It's okay to admit that we are not quite ready for some of our dreams to come true, and it's nice to have a picture of what is possible for us when we are. Once we have a picture, it will continue to work on us and get us ready for it because Life is about expansion and always desiring to experience more. We are the way that IT can do that. We are IT's avenue of expression in the physical world. This is an exercise in working with our intuition. There is that within us that is one with the Universal Mind, which knows everything we will ever need to know. All the knowledge that exists is available to us if we just believe it.

Is there any question I would like to ask before going to bed?

_____

_____

_____

_____

_____

What is something I would like to know?

_____

_____

_____

_____

What do I need to know about this particular person, situation, or experience?

_____

_____

_____

_____

_____

_____

Dreams

Dreams are amazing downloads of information that let us know where we are, or what is going on that we can't quite see or understand in our awake state. If we can learn how to wake up slowly and focus on remembering them, they will provide us with information about where we stand. The more we do this, the more we learn how to decipher them. Our dreams can give us a read on where we are.

Dreams are also ways for us to connect with others, including our loved ones—those who are still alive as well as those who have passed on. These encounters seem to be more than just dreams. I had one of these three weeks after my mother passed away. A group of family members were gathered around in a large living room. It seemed like we were all at a party.

Then I saw her come out of one of the bedrooms. I immediately went to her, and we sought out some privacy in her room. She was so radiantly beautiful. I was relieved and assured that she had achieved something very special. We just gazed at one another, smiling. I was in awe of her glow. In her new enlightened state, I felt closer to her than we had ever been, and we had been close. We embraced, and whatever unfinished business there might have been between us now meant nothing. We were completely resolved with one another. I knew she was back in my life, in a non-physical way that bonded us together forever. She is now a loving presence I can feel all the time. Many mornings I wake up realizing that we have just had time together.

Do I give enough significance to my dreams?

_____
_____
_____
_____
_____
_____

How could I learn more about them?

_____
_____
_____
_____
_____
_____

What dreams do I remember that had an impact on me?

_____
_____
_____
_____
_____
_____

These activities: breathing, pausing for a moment to re-group; appreciating silence; being present to those around us; living in the now moment of power; meditating; asking questions and waiting for answers; and paying attention to our dreams don't sound like much in the way of a spiritual exercise program, but they are worth their weight in gold.

Getting ourselves in circulation through movement is huge. Giving thanks, living in gratitude for our lives and for others, and journaling as a way of keeping track of our progress are all excellent ways to start our spiritual regime.

Getting rid of the clutter, detoxing and forgiveness are perfect ways to release blocks and free up energy, allowing more good to come into our lives. These exercises prepare us to use a power and a presence that goes beyond us in order to move mountains. We are now ready to proceed to strength training, our core exercises.

Personal Journal Notes

_____

_____

_____

_____

_____

_____

_____

_____

_____

_____

_____

_____

_____

_____

Part 2

Dailies/Core/Strength Training

The 4th Way: Imagine

The Truth that sets you free is that you can experience in imagination what you desire to experience in reality, and by maintaining the experience in imagination, your desire will become an actuality.

~ Neville Goddard

Ten years ago, I discovered I had trouble getting up from one of those low-to-the-ground beach chairs. I was much too young to be experiencing what I did. I felt like I was falling apart! As the Infinite Intelligence of Life would have it, my husband had just begun using a fitness coach. John knew exactly what I needed. He wasted no time teaching me exercises on the beach that would strengthen my core. Without that core strength we grow old before our time and physically limited in so many ways. Today, those exercises continue to be a vital part of my regular physical workouts. Because of them my body feels stronger than ever, and I can do things I couldn't do before, ever!

The exercises described below have that same importance and will help us to achieve a maximum level of spiritual strength needed to live boldly... an inspired life without steroids or any other chemicals.

The Power of Intention

One Sunday the youth program at our center taught the difference between wishing and knowing... they went outside and blew bubbles, which represented their intentions. Their intentions quickly flew out of sight into the heavens. What a brilliant exercise to help us all see what happens when we activate the creative process by setting an intention! Our ideas go forth from us, and immediately something new is set into motion as a result. Knowing this is much more powerful than wishing for something to happen. Looks like we need the visual of making more bubbles to take our own intending to the next level!

Playing make believe as a child has the same effect of "acting as if" and expanding our imagination at the same time. Using our imagination is a powerful way to begin the creation process.

Wayne Dyer wrote a wonderful book called *The Power of Intention*. Intention, or intending, is a powerful spiritual practice. Before starting the day, we can ask ourselves, "What is my intention for this day?" or "What do I want to accomplish with this phone call, this meeting... this interaction?"

John and I used to ask our son before he left for school, "What kind of day are you going to have?" Most of the time, he would say, "A fun day." He probably was just saying it to appease his parents. That's okay, because it made him stop and think. Depending on what was going on, he would change it up every now and then to include something more specific, like "Enjoy good friends."

Asking ourselves, "What is my intention?" gives us time to think about what we want to accomplish and how we want to *be*. That's right; we get to play a significant role in how segments of our day--and even our entire day--play out. How do we want to feel during the process and especially at the close? What is the intended result? Instead of assuming that things are going to go well on their own or leaving things up to the law of averages(meaning we win some and lose some), we can choose to put ourselves in the driver's seat and co-create with the Infinite the best possible outcome for all involved. Experiences are sure to go better if *we* are more prepared than if we just wing it. "Hard to have" conversations are easier if our intentions are genuine and we desire loving outcomes for all. If we come from an open, loving place, not only will our results be better, we won't have to look backend wish things could have been different. Sound like too much work? Think of how much energy it takes to regret something that didn't go so well. We spend years wishing we could change things. How much of our energy is wasted that way? Setting an intention will yield maximum solutions. That's using our precious energy in a productive and satisfying way.

One of our students reviewed her intentions for a class she took. It was to live her best life.

I looked back and asked myself what was the major ingredient to living that way? The most important essential ingredient was to follow my heart.

My daughter was in preschool and the school was breaking up. There was a split and some people wanted to go off another way. I decided to follow my heart and it was one of the best decisions I have ever made, and it turned out to be one of the best years of my life.

It was not only the best year for me, it was the best year for my whole family. My husband and I still talk about how great it was. My daughter got one of the best teachers she could have gotten and found her first best friend. I found new, fun, learning games to help my son move forward with his life. My husband and I found a babysitter in the neighborhood and had a fabulous time every Saturday night. All of these things flowed from the decision to follow my heart.

What a beautiful reminder that following our heart will open up new vistas! For her, it all began with setting an intention.

Setting an intention is getting as much consciousness as possible behind an encounter so that we may enjoy a richer, fuller experience. Doing this puts us in a co-creative role with the Universe instead of a reactionary one. When we set our intention, the Universe gets to work and shows up in the most interesting ways.

Here is an example:

My intention for this week is for Spirit to have some fun through me and all those around me. I want to enjoy this time and I know I am supported. I want to lighten up and know that Spirit makes a very special and meaningful meeting for us all. My work load is light. I play my part and know the right and perfect people step up to play the rest of the parts. Together we work as one in perfect synchronicity. Love abounds. It is truly a celebration of Life and all that is good. Thank You, God!

Since we live in a different state I seldom could be a part of all the things that were happening with my birth family. I wanted to do more, but I didn't know how I could. One day, my brother Joe mentioned he had a weekly date with our mother. At once I claimed the idea and incorporated it into my life. Every Monday at 2:00 p.m. my mother and I had a phone date that ended with a prayer for her about whatever she wanted. It was a rewarding way for us to stay connected.

When my mother became ill, my brothers and sister did a superb job taking care of her and her home. When she passed away, it was difficult for any of us to do what needed to be done: clean out her belongings. Even though family members had taken what they wanted, there were still lots of things that needed to be tossed out or given away. It was only fair that I schedule a few uninterrupted days by myself in her home so I could help accomplish the goal.

I treasured that time immensely, including all the memories that came up for me. I savored my last time being there and made sure to make the most of it. I knew I had three days before flying home. I prepared by making a list of intentions beforehand. Here is what I came up with:

- Say goodbye to and release Mom's house.
- See and connect with my brothers and sister and their families.
- Pack and help do physical things that need to be done.
- Clear the house for the next family and welcome them in(symbolically speaking).
- Continue and complete another part of my own grieving process.
- Communicate with Mom.

When I reviewed them after my trip, every one of them had been satisfied. I couldn't believe my eyes...all of this was accomplished! Most of all, I felt my part was complete in fulfilling the mission and hopefully provided some relief for my family as well.

What is my intention for today?

_____

_____

_____

_____

What is my intention for this meeting? This conversation? With this person?

_____

_____

_____

_____

What is my intention for my life?

_____

_____

_____

_____

_____

_____

_____

_____

_____

Visualization

What is visualization? It is another core-building exercise. Visualization is: Simply picturing how we want things to be. It's using your imagination and stretching your mind to think about what is possible. Taking time to fantasize, daydream or pretend what your life could be. Seeing what some areas of your life might look like in your mind's eye. Seeing your dreams come true in that inner space of your mind. Seeing yourself live in the newly conceived world of your own making. Regularly spending time there, mentally, until the picture becomes a reality in your outer world. This is a great spiritual practice, especially if you know what you want. If you don't know what you want, this practice will take you closer to what that might be. Either way it stretches your imagination muscles, taking you further along than where you began.

Sometimes all we need is a boost of energy, and visualizing can jump-start us to get us moving in the right direction. One very special idea can take us places we've never dreamed. Once the mind is expanded, there is no going back! That's a good thing.

Before moving to Central Florida, I tried to sell my condo in Atlanta myself. I had co-owned properties with my first husband, so I knew a few things about selling houses. This, though, was the first time I was on my own. I started by putting a sign out by the road. To my surprise, quite a few people stopped by to look. Not one of them said, "I want it."(Thank God they didn't because I had no paperwork or lawyer in place that could help make the sale, if they had wanted to buy it!)Okay, now what do I do? I had no idea how to accomplish the next step. This went on for a week or so. In my frustration, I mentioned it to my teacher, Dr. Kennedy Shultz, hoping for some insight on the subject from a metaphysical point of view. I was still thinking maybe I could magically sell it myself. (Yes, I was naïve.) "Get an expert to do it. They know what they're doing," he said rather bluntly.

I hadn't really been open to that idea because I had been trying to bypass a realtor. I knew I could only get so much for the place, and I badly wanted to pay off my debts with my proceeds. I didn't see how I could afford a commission and accomplish all of that, too.

I was defining how *I thought* it had to play out. Instead, I needed to focus on the result – which was the sale of my condo, my debts paid, and the feeling of relief that would allow me to move on with the next chapter of my life – and then let the Universe figure out the *how*.

When I tried to make it all happen by myself, not much happened. In fact, there was no movement until I asked for help. Only then did things begin to shift in my favor.

Having professional help was so supportive and freeing that I was able to demonstrate the sale of my condo, payment of my debts, *and* closing that chapter of my life. I was then free to focus my energies on what I wanted to experience in my new life.

That's exactly what I had said I wanted. I just needed to get out of the way, trust, take the action steps I knew to take (like get the condo ready and find a realtor, who conveniently lived right next door), and *know* it was happening in my mind until I saw the actual contract in my hand. This experience served me well in gaining a greater understanding of how to work with the Universe and demonstrate more of what I want.

Imagining a natural spring is a powerful visualization. There are many scenic springs in Florida. In fact, there are more springs in Florida than anywhere else in the world. Each one of them is uniquely and spectacularly beautiful. Some people call them boils because the water can be seen bubbling up from beneath the ground.

Here is a visualization we can experiment with to get the full image of the spring and its effects...

> *Take a moment now, and picture a downpour of rain steadily coming down, watering the plant life, giving drink to the animals, and being absorbed by layer after layer of earth. Then, imagine these gallons and gallons of water filling up the aquifer so much that the water makes its way back up to the surface in a powerful surge...a continuous bubbling up of water. Imagine that for a second.*
>
> *Now, imagine within yourself that same constant bubbling up of energy, love and goodness in place of the water. It's never ending. Make believe you are being fed, supported, guided and directed. It's a constant bubbling up of Spirit within us, all the time. It cannot be stopped.*
>
> *How does that feel? That's an example of something we can do for ourselves. Whenever we feel cut off, whenever we feel alone, all we have to do is:*
>
> *Keep imagining that bubbling up of love within us...the bubbling up of the life force... that endless source of energy that keeps on coming...that unconditional love that knows no end. It just takes over us. It takes over in our bodies. It takes over in our lives. It refreshes us. It cleans and clears us. It transforms our minds. That energy just keeps on coming to the degree that we recognize its presence and allow ourselves to enjoy it.*

Visualization is very powerful. Knowing that the Universe reads our mental pictures, our intentions, and our hearts, and that it creates from there, we can see how important it is to focus on the things we want instead of what we don't want. IT will take them either way, so we may as well choose that which brings us joy. We do this unknowingly all the time, but when we consciously do it we direct energy in a way that is productive and reaps the kind of result we want, or at least gets us started in the process of seeing our next steps. Getting clarity on what we want as we go helps bring into view what we want to see.

One of my students put her own spin on the idea of visualization: "Okay Universe, I'll give you a rough sketch. You fill in the colors."

Genevieve Behrend[3] put it this way:

The exercising of visualizing, the visualizing faculties, keep your mind in order and attract to you the things you need to make life more enjoyable in an orderly way. If you train yourself in the practice of deliberately picturing your desire and carefully examining your picture, you will soon find that your thoughts and desires proceed in a more orderly procession than ever before. Having reached a state of order and totality, you are no longer in a constant state of hurry. Hurry is fear and consequently destructive.

In other words, while your understanding grasps the power to visualize your heart's desire and hold it with your will, it attracts to you all things requisite to the fulfillment of that picture, by the harmonious vibration of the law of attraction. You realize since order is heaven's first law and visualization places things in their natural order, then it must be a heavenly thing to visualize... Visualizing is the great secret of success.

A woman came to Genevieve Behrend for help. She needed to sell some property and didn't know what to do. Genevieve instructed her to:

- mentally picture the sale;
- go through the details of that sale in your mind...all the way through the process of having the property sold; and
- imagine what the *having of it* will mean to you and those around you. (more emotional buy-in).

This woman did what she was instructed to do, and as she was walking down the street, got an idea to see a certain real estate

[3] The Mental Science of Thomas Troward: Your Invisible Power, 1951

person that she normally wouldn't have dealt with. She didn't even really believe he could help her, but she followed the guidance she was given anyway and sought him out. As it turned out, he was the right one to help her, and sold her property within three days.

The woman did not have to figure out the *how*. She didn't have to figure out the order or all the steps that led up to the sale. She did have to let go of the idea of how she would have done it, keep her focus, and concentrate on what she wanted, just like I did in selling my condo.(I also learned that it was helpful to continue living my life and making future plans instead of putting everything on hold until the sale was complete.) There was a definite order in the way things came together to reach the desired goal. The Universe did the ordering of how things came together, step by step.

There are some things that we do know how to do that are simple. They are second nature to do. Those are the things we can do something about. There are other things we don't know what to do with. Those are the things we need to let the Universe handle. Our Source knows all things. There is nothing IT can't do if we will only work with IT.

I mentally picture my desire to:

_____
_____
_____
_____
_____
_____
_____
_____
_____

I see _____

_____

happening.

The fulfillment of this desire would mean this to me:

_____

_____

_____

_____

_____

That demonstration would mean this to the others involved:

_____

_____

_____

_____

_____

_____

Visioning

Visioning is a wonderful spiritual exercise created by Michael Beckwith (more information and specifics about his technique can be found in his books and videos). It is a beautiful way of letting Spirit speak to us.

The visioning process is helpful when we don't really know what we want or when we would like the greater Intelligence within to reveal to us what IT wants to do in, as and through us. This omniscient, omnipotent, omnipresent Intelligence knows everything and easily knows whatever is of interest to us and makes us happy. Why wouldn't we seek out and listen to wisdom and guidance from an Infinite Creator?

In visioning we put forth our questions and then listen. "I am open to the greater wisdom that is trying to happen, or that would like to happen."We are seeking a picture like we would in visualization. In this scenario we are not giving or putting out a specific picture as our starting place. Our desire is to have an idea revealed to us that is *greater* than we can imagine. We are allowing one to come to us. We may have a need to fulfill but have no idea what that looks like because we want more than we, personally, know how to achieve or are unsure what is best for us. We go to a deeper place within ourselves because we seek clarity to that which is still vague.

Specifically, we are asking:

- What does Spirit want to express or experience through and as us in the way of our expression, our path, our relationships, our physical location or dwelling, our health, our wealth?
- What does that look like and feel like?
- What strengths do I bring to the situation?
- What do I need to release so this can happen?
- What do I need to embrace?
- Is there anything else I need to know?

In visioning, we work to keep our limited, conscious mind out of the process and open ourselves up to the greater Mind, the one that can effortlessly bring us new information on the spot. We don't have to make something happen or put effort into thinking hard. We just need to listen to our intuition, the wisdom of our higher Self.

After asking the questions (which may or may not yield immediate results) we just let all that sit for a while and go about our regular life. Putting something on the proverbial "back burner" of our mental stove and letting the subject matter simmer guarantees that something is bound to show up. Many times, we can be doing something totally different, like washing dishes or driving, when an idea pops into our awareness. We are preoccupied with something else, which is a good thing because we are open and receptive in those moments. Our doubts, worries and concerns have been put aside.

Then, after a while, suddenly, something flashes across our mind about the topic we had set aside. Maybe we receive an unexpected invitation, or someone else tells us something about their own experience which relates to our inquiry. A light bulb goes on. Something they say gets our attention and gives us an idea. Time to sit up and take notice. It's exciting and fun to experience this, and when it happens we welcome it happening even more.

We don't always recognize the answers at first, but with practice we can pick up on things more quickly and easily. Through practice we grow in our sensitivity and learn to recognize the subtle messages we would have missed before. It's a big Universe out there! There's much more here than we know. However, ideas come and when they do—and they will—we can be sure Intelligence is working by our side. We have been heard. We have initiated contact with all the Power of the Universe and IT is ready.

If things are a bit slow in coming, there may be something we need to release first. There may be something we need to accept or embrace. One woman knew what strengths or gifts she brought to the table for her desire. When she asked the question, "What do I need to embrace?" she got the answer, *worthiness*. This was her clue. For this demonstration to be successful, she needed to work on her own self-worth so that she could receive. This is the part she needed to play to guarantee a more successful demonstration.

It's perfectly okay if not much is revealed to us at first. Glimpses, insights or even mental pictures may come to us days later. The important thing is that we go through the process, giving it our best focus. We have to begin somewhere, and there is no greater beginning place than to approach our creations spiritually, opening a door to new possibilities we may not have thought about on our own. New variations of what we have seen in the past or entirely new solutions are possible. We live, breathe and have our being in a field of infinite possibility. Why not tap into different, never-before realized ideas that could change life as we know it?

Whatever it is, the process of visioning will help us get some movement going in our minds about the topic in question. This is an exercise in working with our intuition. It works so well because our greater mind can come through when we get out of the way. We do that by recognizing and allowing a greater Intelligence and wisdom to reveal more. There is that within us that is one with the Universal Mind and connects us to IT. Why not take advantage of this greater Intelligence that is available to us?

We don't normally ask ourselves open-ended questions, specifically directed to our higher Self, or the Higher Power and Presence. This is a very powerful tool because it gets us thinking in a different way and opens us up to a whole other world...the spiritual one. It's asking Spirit, "What do *You* want to be as me?

What do *You* want to experience in my finances, in the way of relationships, in the way of my career, or in any other area?" These questions put us into alignment with something so much more exciting and interesting.

I am receptive to something greater than I can imagine regarding

_____

_____

_____

_____

_____

_____

I am open to listening to my higher self in this situation:

_____

_____

_____

_____

_____

_____

Visioning: Team Project #1

This visioning exercise can also be used for a project. In our spiritual center, we used the visioning process for all three of our food packaging events for outreach. We knew very little about how to host one and all that would be needed. We knew we needed all the help we could get. We decided to make sure we were covered spiritually first. This kind of event requires quite a bit of money upfront to pay for all the food needed for the packaging. We had never raised money before for a project outside of the regular support of our center.

The economy had just collapsed and many people in our area lost their homes, so most of the food we packaged was used locally. We envisioned what we wanted to experience, how we wanted to feel about it and generally, how things would go. How could we look at raising money in a way that was fun, creative and drew people wanting to participate? Instead of feeling sorry for those without, how could we uplift them and give in a way that empowered us all? Where could we hold such an event? We got into the feeling of what it would mean to us and to those who were going to receive those meals. What kind of experience was that going to be for our people and for the greater Orlando community that wanted to participate with us?

We drew from a deeper place within for our creation, and it made all the difference. After we wrapped our minds around the idea of what we wanted to create, we began to get ideas about who to contact for the other necessary items for the event. One by one, solutions came to the forefront and it was easy to see we were being divinely led. It was the easiest thing to do because of this process. Each one of us had to ask ourselves: What can I do to make this an exceptional experience? What doubts, fears or reservations do I have that could get in the way of our community event? We had to admit whatever they were so they could be addressed. Certain individuals had to release their doubt about where we were going to get the money. As each person said their part, others added, "You know, I could have said that as well." Every angle was skillfully covered by us all as we followed Spirit's lead and acted together as one mind. Once we knew what the blocks or hesitations were, we could know a greater Truth.

Visioning: Team Project #2

One food packaging event was held in Maitland, just outside of Orlando, under a large donated tent in the parking lot of the Qdoba Mexican Grill restaurant. Packaging required putting together specific measurements of bulk rice, beans, flavorings and vitamins to make a healthy, complete meal. The recipe was originally designed for malnourished children in Africa, whose dietary needs are much different from ours.

In the visioning process, we saw a sunny day. Even though we would be packing the food inside a very large tent, completed boxes waiting for pickup needed to be stacked outside. It could not rain.

As we got closer to our big day, questions continued to surface about what we were going to do if it rained. "What is Plan B?" we were asked over and over. It was close to December, when we typically get more precipitation. Our team would reply, "There is no Plan B. It's going to be a sunny day. It's going to be perfect. It's going to be an absolutely great day for packaging food. In fact, it is already a success." That is how we answered the question and how we reinforced the mental image we were creating in our own minds.

The day arrived and it was sunny. It could be that it would have been a sunny day anyway. It no longer mattered; we got what we needed.

That's an example of what's possible. It could have been a catastrophe, but I believe we would have been directed otherwise, and a backup location would have been available to us. Since we were getting no such information, we stood our ground. Our intention was genuine. Everything was in place and we were ready to go. We got what we needed.

Within a period of 18 months, our small but mighty community raised close to $20,000 for food during three unique events and donated nearly 100,000 meals to the Second Harvest Food Bank in Central Florida. We were most grateful, not only for what we were able to share but for the opportunity to work together as a cohesive team. We grew and expanded spiritually in tremendous ways from those experiences. I don't believe we could have accomplished all of that without the visioning process.

Visioning is a powerful process to do by yourself and is most definitely useful in building spiritual muscles. It is also a stellar creation process to do with others. Either way, it is a great first step when taking on anything new and different. Visioning can take us to new heights and clear the way for something greater to happen. Who doesn't want more of that?

You cannot stay on the summit forever; you have to come down again... So why bother in the first place? Just this:

What is above knows what is below, but what is below does not know what is above... One climbs, one sees. One descends, one sees no longer, but one has seen. There is an art of conducting oneself in the lower regions

*by the memory of what one saw higher up. When one can
no longer see, one can at least still know.*
> ~ René Daumal in *Compass Points* by Frank Henninger

How can I use the visioning process in my own life?

_____
_____
_____
_____
_____
_____
_____

What areas of my life could I use it for?

1. _____
   _____
2. _____
   _____
3. _____
   _____
4. _____
   _____

We are working with an Infinite Intelligence which designed the Universe. There is an order to how things come into being. In the sequence of events that take place, certain things are necessary before other steps can be achieved. Things are always created in mind before they can ever come into form. Things can't come before they're ready. Sometimes we aren't ready, even though we think we are. It helps to know what's going on.

When we grow impatient for something to happen or ask why we aren't seeing evidence of it happening, we can know something is always happening. There is an order to the way things unfold. When we know this, we can relax and do what is ours to do, what we know needs to be done. We can get more involved in the details, preparing ourselves and those around us to be ready for when it does come together. When we do this, we become a stronger magnetic force calling our good into being. We can enjoy the adventure, knowing full well the manifestation is underway. The more experience we have in doing this, the more quickly we can believe that this is how the Universe works and expedite the process.

Setting an intention, visualization, and visioning are all excellent ways to exercise our spiritual muscles by using our imaginations.

Personal Journal Notes

_____

_____

_____

_____

_____

_____

_____

_____

_____

_____

_____

_____

The 5th Way: Create

Our relationship to thought is everything. It's what determines how free we will be to create our own destiny and to consciously participate in the evolutionary process.

~ Alan Cohen

Anyone who loves their thoughts greatly and loves their words greatly is sure to be a musician of some kind. There is much joy in their lives, too, as they continually experience the song of the Spirit in their thoughts and words.

~Ruth L Miller, on the work of Emma Curtis Hopkins

Words are clear indicators of the heart's beliefs: what the heart feels and believes, our words are sure to speak, and our experience to follow.

~Ruth L Miller, on the work of Emma Curtis Hopkins

Affirmations

Affirmations are a great spiritual practice. Just one or two powerful lines that declare what we know to be true, or what we would like to believe as possible, can turn our thinking around in an instant. They are as powerful as a mantra (a powerful phrase said over and over in our minds to soothe us and keep us focused on a new idea). We can say them throughout the day or whenever we get caught up in surrounding conditions or a negative mindset. They are instant pick-me-ups. They work quickly to change our focus and shift our thinking.

My first experience with affirmations was in my late 20s when I started working in sales. I really struggled with the idea of saying words like, "I am a top salesperson" when clearly, I wasn't even close. The truth was I didn't have a clue as to what I was doing. It was too big a leap to go from no experience to seeing myself as successful. My competitive nature knew that was a goal I wanted to attain, but I was far from feeling accomplished. I felt like I was lying about myself to myself, let alone others, to even say those words. Affirmations went against everything I was taught growing up. Besides feeling like a lie, it seemed presumptuous to claim something before it came true. Even more, I didn't want to jinx it from ever happening. This was my first exposure to learning how to work with my mind in a positive way to get better results. Thank God I persisted! Looking back, I can say sales broke me into a positive way of looking at things through affirmations.

My next experience with affirmations was reading a metaphysical book by Catherine Ponder, *The Dynamic Laws of Prosperity*. Her inspiring stories back up the importance of using powerful affirmations. I used her suggested affirmations to get me out of some very unpleasant conditions, one of which involved a temporary position I had in an office with two cutthroat lawyers. My absolute favorite was:

> *Your circumstances may be uncongenial, but they shall not long remain so if you perceive an ideal and strive to reach it. You cannot travel within and stand still without.*

I clung to these words. They spoke to my soul. I repeated them until I was certain they were true for me.

I could see and feel my mindset changing. My inner world was moving and there was good reason to believe something dynamic was about to burst in my outer world. My thinking was more positive than ever. A spark was lit in me that had been dim for a very long time. I enjoyed a renewed confidence in myself as I received new insights and perspectives...thoughts I never had before. Even though I couldn't see changes on the outside happening yet, I trusted that changes were on their way. They soon came in the form of a saner, more stable work environment. Praise God!

The biggest payoff was learning how to work *with* Life instead of against it. I was just beginning to get the hang of a whole new way of living my life. I was ready to take on other areas of my life that needed an upgrade. Affirmations supported me as I moved into a brand-new life.

Next, I started reading affirmations from the *Creative Thought* magazine, a Science of Mind publication. I was informed that reading affirmations out loud made them more powerful. I decided to try reading some aloud before leaving for work. At first, I stumbled on the words. It's not easy to mouth strong words of Truth when we've never said them before. There is an energy behind them that is precise, clear, and to the point. Slowly, with practice, I began to find my voice and say them in the privacy of my own home.

While attending a class, I met a guy who later became a good friend and running partner. At the time we were studying *You Can Heal Your Life* by Louise Hay. On nights when we ran after work together, Jeff would powerfully yell out affirmations from Louise's book as we ran through the streets of Midtown, in Atlanta. He didn't care who heard! I was embarrassed at first and remained timid about shouting these statements for all to hear. He was fearless and led them for a long time.

One day Jeff turned to me and said, "It's your turn!" I said, "I can't do this." He gave me a look. Meekly, I made my first awkward attempts. It took some time for me to get comfortable using my outside voice for all to hear. I will forever be grateful to Jeff for helping me get over myself. Soon it became second nature to me, too. I got to the point where I couldn't run without affirming something that would help me. I admit, it was an electrifying experience to feel the affirmations vibrate through my being!

Jeff also supported me in running races, the most famous of which was Fourth of July Peachtree Road Race. Shortly after we began, we got my good friend and co-worker, Carol, to get in on the action. In no time at all, she was running with us and affirming. It was an incredible workout! To this day, I am thankful to Jeff for our precious time together, running and affirming. He was a great influence on me and my future. He helped me break out of myself, and he showed me an example of what a spiritual man looks like. He played a huge part in the future demonstration of my life partner, John.

Affirmations are helpful one-liners that really speak to us. When they touch us in a strong way, they can be quite effective in expanding consciousness. I went to a workshop where we created one by using a formula. I can't remember the process now, but I use the one I created to this day: *joyfully express the freedom of spirit!*

It's great to memorize the ones we love and carry them in our back pocket for those times of need. Affirmations have been part of a process that I have used through the years. I have grown to love them very much because they are simple, yet impactful. As we invest in ourselves through regular practice, phenomenal growth can occur. We just start where we are and keep on going. See where it all leads. Affirmations are most effective in building our spiritual muscles.

What are some of my favorite quotes, mantras, and inspiring words?

1. _____

2. _____

3. _____

4. _____

5. _____

What can I affirm now for myself?

1. _____

2. _____

3. _____

4. _____

5. _____

What can I affirm now to attract my greater good?

1. _____
   _____
2. _____
   _____
3. _____
   _____
4. _____
   _____

Afformations

An affirmation, or an *afformation*, is a positive statement which creates. *Af-form-ation* contains the word *form*. We are creating a physical reality or form with this kind of statement or question.

Afformations is a concept created by Noah St. John and described in greater detail in his book, *The Book of Afformations*. Afformations are a variation of affirmations: affirmations put as a question:

* Why?
* Why am I so wealthy now?
* Why am I so successful now?

It changes the emphasis to already possessing what we desire in our mind before we see it. Typically, affirmations are done from a place of wanting and not having. Afformations give the practice a twist which strengthens our position.

Affirmation: *I am healthy and strong.*
Afformations:
* Why am I healthy and strong?
* Why am I so healthy and strong?

Affirmation: *I am financially prosperous.*
Afformations:
* Why am I financially prosperous?
* Why am I so financially prosperous?

It's a great concept because it tells us we've already shifted our consciousness to the idea that we are healthy and strong or financially prosperous.

Asking why gives the Universe, or Creative Spirit of Life, an opportunity to show us the reasons we already are. This further impacts our consciousness with the idea that we have already achieved our desire, which convinces us and makes the demonstration happen more quickly. This is a very effective alternative to affirmations. This technique and expanded explanation can be found in St. John's books and videos, offered by Hay House.

What afformations can I use that would be effective for me?

1. _____
2. _____
3. _____
4. _____
5. _____

Why am I _____?

Why am I so _____?

Ideal Day

My husband, John, and I recently saw a spectacular whale jumping out of the water in all its magnificence and glory – in a life insurance commercial. It really caught our eye seeing this huge being dive into the depths, full tail fins displayed. That happens to be a thing for me. I have a picture of tail fins right smack in the middle of my vision board to remind me always to go deeper for answers in order to live a richer, fuller life. Sometimes we have to stop looking at surface information and dive deeper to get our answers.

A client, knowing how special that idea is to me, gave me a bracelet with a charm of the tail fins on it. Another close friend blessed me with a replica of the tail fins for my office coffee table.

What we focus on, we demonstrate. Whatever leaves an impression on our consciousness demonstrates in the real world.

My love for this idea and making it a special spiritual reminder to me brought it into view on our TV for me to further enjoy. The subconscious powerfully picks up on whatever we give our attention to. That means we can be selective about what we wish to experience by carefully choosing our thoughts.

I had totally forgotten that my fascination with whales actually began much earlier, when John and I shared an ideal day in our early years together. Recently married, we were on our way to the Asilomar grounds in Pacific Grove for a week-long conference with the Centers for Spiritual Living. We flew into San Francisco to stay with a friend before driving down. When we arrived at the car rental counter, they asked if we wanted an upgrade at no extra charge. We looked at each other and didn't hesitate to say, "Yes!" It turned out to be this gorgeous, aqua blue Chrysler Sebring convertible. We were ecstatic! Then I remembered it was quite cold outside. John wasted no time at all and said, "That's okay. We will just turn the heat on." And that is what we did.

While we toured San Francisco, we made a point of visiting the Ghirardelli Chocolate Factory to pick up a few things for the road.

The day we left was a perfectly beautiful sunny day. We drove down the Pacific Coast Highway enjoying our good fortune, happier than ever. We didn't think the day could get any better. To our surprise there was much more for us to see and enjoy. Almost at once, we spotted a large humpback whale jumping out of the water, off in the distance. This was our first such sighting. We had never seen something so amazing in the wild. It was breathtaking to behold such a spectacular view! Clearly this powerful creature was expressing joy. What else could it be?

As it turns out, the whale was on a similar path down the coast as we were, which meant we were able to catch it in action a few more times as we traveled south. We loved every minute we had with our whale partner and greatly appreciated the fabulous show it put on just for us. We had a car that allowed us to take in all the luscious countryside and oceanside as we drove, plus we had chocolate! It was heavenly! Truly, this was an ideal day if ever there was one!

Years later the whale's tail became a symbol that reminds me to go deeper when I need guidance and inspiration.

I know everyone's idea of heaven is not the same. For some, it would look quite different. Of course, not all days are as ideal as that special day was for us, but they definitely can be more to our liking than we think they can. We can make something more of our day that meets our personal specifications. Learning how to manage our day is huge because each individual day makes up our life. We can let our days be whatever they will be and let them have a mind of their own, or we can take an active part in attracting to them elements that are special to us. Instead of "run of the mill" days, we can customize them more to our liking.

How do we do that?

Every morning we can jot down the essence of what we would like to experience for that day. If mornings are not the best time, we can pick another time during the day. Evenings can be a great time to relax and create, depending on our energy and focus at that time of day. We want to give this exercise our best love and attention because this will literally help us create the kind of day we want to experience, the kind of relationships we want to have, the kind of work we want to do, how much good we want to enjoy, how we want to experience ourselves, and how we want to feel through it all. This exercise encompasses all those separate components that could make up our entire day, just like setting an intention for what we would like to see happen. This is an expansion of that practice, an opportunity to get into the consciousness of our desire and do the necessary "behind the scenes" work.

Emma Curtis Hopkins, a powerful teacher of the early 20th century, said it this way: "Everyday, take time to sit and write. Name your good."

Our thoughts are creative. They are like a signal being broadcast that will manifest in physical form, to be played in the future. The more proficient we become with this, the more quickly we will see things happen. This is a great way to co-create with the Universe and live every day to the fullest. I have used this practice for more than a decade now, and it continues to make a huge difference in my life. It helps me remember that I am a powerful creator. When I stay in creation, I actively see my interplay with Life many times throughout the day. This daily work builds as I go and supports me in being all I can be so that I can really enjoy the creation of the huge garden I call my life.

All we do is name our good and stay focused. We watch to see how some days go and decide the next day what we are finished with and what we want to see more of. Every day is an opportunity to start over and make our days more to our liking, for our own pleasure and for the enjoyment of those around us.

Below is a further explanation for each of the steps, followed by a form titled "Ideal Day" for your personal use. An additional copy of the form can be found in the Addendum section of this workbook.

> **My Ideal Day is filled with**... We list qualities we would like to experience that we may not be currently feeling. In this step, we set the intention for our day, for example:
> * Peace,
> * Love,
> * Courage,
> * Vibrant Health,
> * Confidence,
> * Wisdom,
> * Guidance.
>
> **I am...** We list statements, affirmations, reminders of who we are. These are statements about our inner being that fortify us as we begin to identify with them, like:
> * I am love.
> * I am peace.
> * I am spirit.
> * I am vibrant health and wholeness.
> * I am rich beyond measure.
>
> **I let Spirit, or Universe, in me and around me, know that I am ready to experience the following:** This is where we list more specifically what we want to experience today or for a longer-term project we are working on. *Make it so in a special way that only you can.* We basically hand it over and release it to the higher Power. Examples might include:

- I am ready to experience "prime time" with my daughter, son, or friend. I am ready for the successful completion of my project.
- I am ready to experience the energy I need to give my very best to this day.
- I follow my inner guidance and take the next action steps I know to take: Here we list whatever ideas come to us, such as:
  - I listen.
  - I meditate.
  - I make that phone call (that I have been putting off).
  - I clean off my desk.
  - I schedule that appointment.

I AM grateful for... We list statements of appreciation; they are huge attractors which magnify our presence. In order to attract the desires of our heart or those things we want to see, we can be grateful for the blessings we already have, show our appreciation, and keep our vibration high. Gratitude and thanksgiving open our hearts and minds and polish our thoughts.

- I am thankful for inspiration.
- I am grateful in advance for this beautiful day.
- I give thanks for living in the flow.
- I appreciate the love and support of those around me.
- I am grateful in advance for guidance and next steps.
- I AM grateful for the highest and best happening for (others):
- I am grateful for knowing my sons and daughter are supported where they are.
- I am grateful for my aunt who is making her transition at this time; for knowing she is well taken care of right where she is.

I accept and acknowledge that this declaration is becoming my experience...

- I accept this ideal day as I have specified and all that is added to benefit me and my family.
- I wholeheartedly accept all this and more... And so it is!

That's it! This exercise gives a framework for our day and opens the door to creating more of what we want to see.[4]
Try it for yourself:

Date: _____

My ideal day is filled with:

_____
_____
_____
_____

I AM:

_____
_____
_____
_____

SPIRIT, Source, or Universe, in me and around me, I am ready to experience the following:

_____
_____
_____
_____

MAKE IT SO in a special way that only you can.

I follow my inner guidance and take the next action steps I know to take:

1. _____

_____

---

[4] A form for this exercise is in the back of this workbook. Feel free to make copies so you can use it each day.

2. _____
   _____
3. _____
   _____
4. _____
   _____

I AM grateful for:

_____
_____
_____
_____

I AM grateful for highest and best happening for (others):

_____
_____
_____
_____

I WHOLEHEARTEDLY ACCEPT ALL THIS and MORE.
AND SO IT IS!

It doesn't have to take a long time. It gets easier as we get into the flow of it. We can't help but get new ideas as we go. It's also a great idea to review what transpired the day before to see how things might have changed because of a new concept we added. Remembering what happened and comparing it with our notes from the previous day helps us to connect the dots and see the bigger picture that we might otherwise miss. Noticing shifts and changes encourages us to keep practicing so we can see more.

A friend recently told me that she shared this concept and form with some of the people she works with. In a very busy university office, her staff are working diligently to turn things around and are experiencing great success!

Advanced Ideal Days

The Ideal Day exercise can be done as a letter to our Higher Power or as a declaration:

My Ideal Day is filled with enlightened, inspiring experiences. I especially experience the fullness of my being. I see clearly and precisely. I have the courage to embrace my larger vision. I live in Pure Potentiality. I am taken to new heights of awareness and consciousness with demonstrations of Your perfection, God. I fully embrace and realize Your love, my connection to you, the awe of the big picture You have in mind for me, the immensity of what You know and see for what is possible for me. Transformation takes place in every area of my life. I forever release the old strain, struggle, boring details, the mundane and burdensome. I no longer carry them. I am free. I love being free! It feels so good to be me. I celebrate the bigger life You have planned. It was well worth the wait. Thank You, God, for my most extraordinary life, the wonder, beauty, opulence and abundance of it all. I am so blessed now and forever! And so it is!

Another example might be:

My Ideal Day is filled with Fun and Relaxation. I am a creator, and I enjoy the life I have created. I do my best work when I am happy, playful and relaxed. I live this way, and I am happier than ever as I see transformation take place in each and every one of these areas:

I have a closer, more loving relationship, partnership and marriage with John.

I have greater fulfillment, peace and joy in relationship with myself.

I have easier, more mature, relaxed and fruitful relationships with my children.

I have more support than ever in my work. There is more alignment with people working together for our community, doing what we love, and making a difference.

I am attracting greater monies and am generously compensated for my work. I never worry about money again and always have everything I need and more.

I have a beautiful home that serves us perfectly. I love and enjoy it immensely. It allows me the freedom and space to do what I love and to BE.

We have the perfect Center location for our many activities, classes and events.

This all feels good. I accept it all now! All of Life responds and says, "Yes!"

And so it is!

This one almost wrote itself. I just had to put pen to paper and it flowed. I like to call this a download from the Infinite:

My Ideal Day is filled with excitement, purpose, high vibration, energy, clearing and cleaning, order and organization, vision, passion, insight, fun, transformation, beauty, goodness, flow, abundance, perfection, connection, presence, power, vitality, strength, appreciation, support, realization, communion, ecstasy, bliss, divine substance and You, Oh Great Spirit!

My family and I are richer and happier each day. Everyday transformation clarifies me and the picture of my life. Every day it gets clearer, brighter, shinier, easier and more fun. Every day more situations take care of themselves and resolutions take place, freeing us from debts and old responsibilities. It gets easier and easier to support ourselves as we align ourselves with You, our Source, our Substance and Supply. More and more we live in rhythm with You and reap the great benefits of being in the flow. Everyday our picture visibly transforms for the better, and we are encouraged to take bigger leaps into the creative process. Every day we encourage others by living the life of our dreams. Every day, like the phoenix, wearise out of the ashes and more and more we are standing solid and bold, feeling more powerful than ever.

I now see as Spirit sees: Everything is pleasing to my eyes, warms my heart and moves me profoundly. Thank You, Spirit! Thank You, God! Make it all so. I am focused and ready to do my part. I gleefully accept all the wisdom, clarity, happiness, abundance and life-force available to me. I see myself being more successful, doing what I love and happier than ever. I am flooded with everything good just being the divine, magnificent spirit I am, as You.

Mind Treatment

Our ability to commune with the forces of the cosmos, to choose our path through time and determine our course of future history, may be the single most sophisticated and empowering force to grace our world.

~ Gregg Braden

The movie *A Beautiful Mind* was based on the life of John Forbes Nash, Jr., a Nobel Laureate in Economics. Russell Crowe starred as John, the main character with a genius mind who had gone over the edge. At the end of the movie, John walks out of a building and his mind fragments. He sees two figures standing to the side watching him, trying to get his attention. He walks by, engaged in a conversation with others. These two figures are the main characters in his head, originators of the voices he hears. He can't help but notice them because they have been his faithful companions through the years. Even though he is in a much healthier place now, they remain. What's different between now and what he had experienced before? In the past he would have engaged them. Now he chooses to ignore them and keeps on going.

We all have some version of those destructive or negative voices in our minds (devils of our own making that are difficult to ignore). If we continue to listen to them, they will most likely be our destruction. John rose above them, not by pretending they didn't exist and not by giving them their say. He triumphed because he understood that he is not his mind, but the thinker behind the mind. The thinker behind the mind is in the driver's seat and can choose which thoughts to think or not think.

Each one of us has the power to choose at any given time. The opportunity is ours to make the right choices. The best ones make all the difference in the long run. Even when that isn't easy and we continue to hear the voice of fear, the voice of doubt or the voice that says we aren't good enough, we can choose again.

When I think of what my mind is like now compared to what it once was, I am amazed at how far I have come. I know that my mind can only continue to grow in its ability to process and evolve in what it can comprehend. It's typically not something we think about. An undeveloped mind can easily be distracted. A disturbed mind can play an upsetting scene over and over again for weeks, replaying it as if it had just happened. We sometimes relive the conversations we are stuck on until we grow sick and tired. We finally let them go out of exhaustion. I was there myself during a very difficult time. I dwelled on some disturbing arguments for up to three weeks!

There was a student with whom I worked years ago that I couldn't understand. Granted, some of that could have been my inexperience in teaching the subject matter at that time. He would respond to a question, and it was as if he were speaking a different language. He thought he was clear. Something was off. If it wasn't his words, maybe it was his feelings. I don't know. He eventually did become clear as he worked on himself. I was quite relieved to know it wasn't me when I began to see the change. That's where Mind Treatment comes in: *It reorganizes our thought processes so that we can think more clearly, making our thought more powerful and capable in the creation process.*

When I first started attending services and classes at a Center for Spiritual Living, I began to feel better immediately. Just hearing healthy, more loving ideas opened me up to new ways of looking at Life. Being together with others who were open to thinking this way, serious about working on themselves, and wanting to create a better life for themselves encouraged me to do the same. For the first time in a very long time, I was happy! My mental, emotional, physical and spiritual health improved so much in the first two years that I didn't know there was something more I could do to have even greater control over the direction of my life. I remember asking, "You mean there is more?"

Absolutely! There is always more. I didn't know I was about to learn how to use a mental tool that I would depend on daily for the rest of my life, sometimes three to four or more times a day to shift my consciousness, my perspective, my thinking, on the spot to know what I really need to know from a place of Universal Truth, and to know the highest possible thoughts about myself and others in any and all situations. This was the practice for me!

I had experienced Mind Treatments given by others on Sundays and done in class as a group. I even went to see a Practitioner to receive my first private treatment and am happy I had the courage to keep that appointment; otherwise I might still be living alone! I wanted to have a loving partner. Rev. Karen Wolfson is the practitioner/minister who helped me with this. Thanks to Karen and treatment, today I share my life with a wonderful man. After many years of being in the ministry, Karen became a very special friend. The treatment she did all those years ago continues to yield a great harvest.

The day I discovered there was more, it dawned on me that I could learn how to do this for myself. It was time for me to learn the process. Once I started learning how to do mind treatments, I felt like shouting, "Watch out world!" My good friend Carol and I would spend hours and hours discussing and writing treatments about what we wanted to create and experience. We were creating consciously for the first time in our lives. As newbies, it was a very exciting time for us.

Not long after John came into my life, she said, "I want a guy just like John." Soon afterward, she demonstrated her own version of John, a nice guy who dearly loves her and is a dedicated husband and father to their son. We had a good laugh, and still do, at how much he even looks like John. Be careful what you ask for, you just might get it!

What is Mind Treatment?

Is treatment something that someone does for us? What does it entail? Is it for everyone? Can someone treat for themselves? What about doing it for others? What's it all about?

These days we get all kinds of treatments: massages, pedicures, reflexology, facials and skin treatments. The list goes on. There are all kinds of things to do for ourselves. Mind Treatment is no different. It can be done for us, and/or it can be done by us, for ourselves and for others.

What do Mind Treatments do? The practice helps us to:
- Center our mind

- Sit in the director's seat
- Clarify our thought processes
- Bring us into alignment with our Source
- Shift consciousness to change our awareness
- Broaden our perspective
- Get a desired result

When most people have a thought, they think that this thought or belief is theirs for keeps. They possess it. It must be a part of them. They hang onto it because they think it defines who they are. Sometimes they are attached to that persona as if their life depends on it. They believe this must be who they are. They are afraid to have their ideas challenged in any way because they believe they are their thoughts. If we believe we are our thoughts, we are going to hold onto them as a way of defending ourselves. But if we believe we are something more than our thoughts, we are free to explore other thoughts and perspectives.

We think that just because we *have a thought,* that must be what we believe. Not necessarily. What most of us don't know is that we are not our beliefs. We are something more than any beliefs we might hold. We hang on to our beliefs because we don't realize that there are many other wonderful ideas and beliefs where those came from. There is an Infinite Mind to tap into which is endless in ITs Intelligence, providing us with possibilities and explanations that go beyond our smaller minds. There is not a problem this Intelligence can't handle. As we get in touch with how Life really works, we will find there are always clearer and better ways to think. Why is this so important to know? It's important because learning how to think means learning how to live. Learning how to live is a skill that can be learned by anyone willing to learn it.

Mind Treatment is really a form of prayer. It is called affirmative prayer because it is made up of definite, positive statements of Truth. It is not begging, bargaining with or beseeching a distant deity who needs convincing and only shows up every now and then. Rather, it is recognizing that:

- God is all there is.
- There is only one Power in the Universe.
- We are one with the Creator of All.

- We are expressions of our Source.
- Life is here to support us.
- Life wants us to succeed.
- Source provides for all of ITs creations.

Mind Treatment is a tool to shift consciousness out of the obvious condition and into the spiritual realm of Truth. It's called treatment because it works with changing our minds and keeping them open. It is truly a spa treatment for the mind. It gets our minds into alignment with Universal Mind, or Spirit. How can that not feel good?

This is an active, alive, conscious communication with Source, the Universe, Life, Spirit... whatever we choose to call God is okay. IT doesn't care. We're not talking to some entity separate from ourselves. We are part of our Creator. We are one with our Source. This form of communication goes beyond prayer as we typically know it. It is not passive like a meditation. Meditation is more of a quieting, a listening, a communing. Some call mind treatment "prayer treatment" to signify that it is, indeed, very much a prayer--a more evolved form of prayer, one that engages us in active, ongoing participation with Life. As we relate intellectually to the Infinite Intelligence of the Universe, we gain access to a wealth of information previously unknown to us, which can lead us to experience extraordinary outcomes. Life becomes much more exciting, and we quickly see that the game of Life is the only real game in town.

Spiritual Mind Treatment was originally designed by Dr. Ernest Holmes, founder of Science of Mind, after his study of world religions, teachings, philosophies and personal experiences. Ancient wisdom supports this kind of prayer, as did the work of Christ Jesus.

It is most often taught as a five-step method, which would exclude steps four and five shown in the example below. It can also be used in one step: gratitude is a bold statement of acknowledgement and appreciation and can be used as a mind treatment entirely on its own because it immediately puts us into a state of alignment with our Source, opening the floodgates to more good for us.

For maximum coverage or when we really need some mind changing or upliftment, I recommend seven steps. It's helpful to be familiar with all seven steps, as some circumstances require more of a shift to take place than others.

Below are 7 Steps to Mind Treatment with more specific explanations for each step. Following that is an example of a mind treatment that can be used as a guide, along with a Mind Treatment form for personal use. An additional form can be found in the Addendum section of this workbook.

7 Steps to Mind Treatment

Focus: Clarity

Step 1: I recognize a higher power.

Step 2: I remind myself that I am *one* with IT.

Step 3: I embody the idea I am creating (health, wholeness, perfection, and abundance...whatever it is).

Step 4: I see what happens to be in my way and release it. I recognize a fear, a doubt, or a sense of giving away my power in a situation, and I release it. I release my doubts about this happening now. I just let them go. Just like in *A Beautiful Mind,* I see them and I keep on going.

Step 5: More strongly than ever, I affirm what I know to be my truth about the situation from the God point of view.

Step 6: I give thanks.

Step 7: I am complete. I release it. And so it is!

Example of a specific Mind Treatment:

Focus: Peace of Mind and Heart

Step 1: Recognition: *I believe in a Universe that is perfect. Peace and harmony reside at the heart of Life.*

Step 2: Unification: *I am one with the Universe. I was created out of peace, love and joy.*

Step 3: Affirmation: *Therefore, peace, love and joy are at the core of my being.*

[optional Step 4: Denial: *Nothing or no one can get in the way of my peace of mind and heart.*]

[optional Step 5: Reaffirmation: *I am peace. I am pure love. I am at peace with myself and the world.*]

Step 6: Gratitude: *I am grateful in advance for the magnificent opportunity to feel and express peace and harmony wherever I go.*

Step 7: Release: *And so it is!*

Writing a Mind Treatment

Topic or Desire (What you want to do, have or be):

_____

_____

_____

Recognition (There's only one creative power, everywhere equally present)

_____

_____

_____

_____

_____

_____

Unification (I am... embodying those same attributes)

_____

_____

_____

_____

_____

Affirmation/Realization (That which I desire has already been given)

_____

_____

_____

_____

_____

_____

Denial (Anything unlike what I desire has no power in itself or in my life)

_____

_____

_____

_____

_____

_____

Reaffirmation (So I can have it)

_____

_____

_____

_____

_____

Gratitude (I'm grateful to know it)

_____

_____

_____

_____

_____

_____

Release (I don't have to know how to do it, I let go, let God figure out the how)

_____

_____

_____

_____

And so it is!

As you go along, you can customize these mind treatments with your own creative ideas and words. Your own mind treatments may be elaborated and personalized if you so desire.

Here's another example:

My Personal Value Expands

I believe in a Power for Good in the universe. It is Infinite Intelligence, Infinite Supply, Infinite Wisdom and Infinite Love.

I was created by this Power. I have complete and direct access to all of IT's good, intelligence, strength and love.

Today, I emphasize my worth to myself and to the world, focusing on my unique talents and abilities, knowing that I am of great value to myself and to those around me. My value continually expands and so does my confidence. My talents and abilities grow magnificently because the Infinite expresses as me.

I take the focus away from concern about where my good is coming from and how all my needs will be met. I release my fears regarding any form of limitation, including the lack of money.

I know that I contribute to the higher consciousness of the universe, to the greater love and good of the universe. The universe needs me and richly supports my intention and purpose.

I give thanks for knowing this perfect truth about myself, my Source and my good.

And so it is!

Regarding treatment outcomes: There's a lot of talk these days about vibrating at a higher energy level in order to more easily manifest our good. We are made of energy. We must first be in tune or aligned vibrationally with what we say we want to see. When we understand that we create our experience, then we can create more of what we want and less of what we don't want. We can't necessarily maintain a high energy level about an idea we would like to see 24/7. We can *know* in our minds and believe in our hearts that whatever we desire is already ours until we see it come into physical form.

Believing is seeing it in our minds before seeing the physical demonstration

Often people say, "I will believe it when I see it." That's not the way things work. Being a universal law, our desire must come into being if we are thinking about it the right way. There is no need to hold thoughts or even send them. *Knowing* is enough. There is no other power working against us. There is only one Power that backs us totally.

Once one has an idea, it is known in Universal Mind immediately. Anyone of us who is receptive to information about a subject has access to it. We are all tapped into this Mind whether we realize it or not. The Universe takes care of the rest. If we *know* that we already have what we want to demonstrate in our mind, then it is already done in the Mind of God or Universal Mind. We are already vibrating on a higher plane and will naturally and easily manifest our heart's desires and all those other things we need to live a creative, wonderful life. Most of all, we will experience ourselves in greater and more expansive ways.

We can't possibly be excited all the time trying to keep our idea alive mentally. We can't generate enough enthusiasm and excitement to last, nor do we need to. We can relax and surrender to the Higher Power that knows how to make it all so. Some ideas take longer to manifest than others. But we can always *know*. When you *know*, you know it's already done. It's a done deal. In the theater of life, we watch it play out. This puts us in a co-creative position with the Infinite. Empowering, isn't it?

What do I already know with all my heart?

_____

_____

_____

_____

_____

_____

What do I *know with all my heart* that I already have?

_____

_____

_____

_____

_____

_____

Partner Up

Spiritual exercise is no different from physical exercise. For staying accountable and building strength, there is nothing like working together with a friend, a co-worker or even a coach.

Prayer/treatment partners can be invaluable to our progress. Personally, I have had a prayer partner for the past 19 years. It all started when a few of us got together to treat/pray for our dear teacher while he underwent a health challenge. Three of us stayed together for some time. Sam and I continued. It has been one of the greatest gifts I have been given by Life, to have someone with whom I can express my deepest thoughts and fears, who loves me no matter what, and who will help take me to a higher place in consciousness when I need it.

Having a spiritual workout partner is a lot like having a physical workout partner. It's inspiring to work with another and it forces us to do more than we would on our own. Accountability can be a very good thing!

What qualities would I like to see in a prayer/treatment partner?

_____

_____

_____

_____

_____

_____

What qualities do I have to offer someone in this kind of relationship?

_____

_____

_____

_____

_____

_____

Do I know someone who might be interested in doing this work together?

_____

_____

_____

Text Messaging

When working with clients who are going through a particularly difficult time, I ask them to text me daily until they feel strong enough to take it from there. The text message includes the following three things:

1. A statement about what they are grateful for in the current day.
2. An affirmative statement about what they expect to see tomorrow, such as, "I affirm that tomorrow is a productive day where I am feeling stronger than ever."
3. Whether or not they are meditating that day (5–10 minutes can really calm us down and open things up for us…sitting in the stillness, listening to our breath, hearing Spirit speak, etc.).

This practice helps us feel a connection to others when we really need it *and* sets up a spiritual practice for us to adhere to everyday, keeping us on track. Just as with running, having a track or route on which to run makes all the difference.

To the best of my ability are my text messages upbeat, positive and uplifting? _____

If not, how can I more consistently move into a loving and supportive role?

_____

_____

_____

_____

_____

_____

Too often, we take life as it comes. Reacting, settling and living by default leave us feeling disempowered: not a way to live. Affirmations, Afformations, Ideal Days, and Mind Treatments are all excellent ways to get us involved in the creative process. We were given great minds with unlimited potential in order that we could master conditions and create things we never dreamed possible. It's true!

These spiritual practices build our spiritual muscles and our ability to create. They put us in the driver's seat and in a co-creative partnership with the Universe that is transformative, which can only make way for new doors to open for us.

Affirmations and Afformations are great places to start. Then, when we are ready, Ideal Days are good to experiment with to see where they might take us. Mind Treatments are the ultimate power-lifting exercises to shift consciousness to a higher place and align us with our Higher Power.

As with anything else, our workouts and the progress and success we achieve depend on our developing ways to keep at it. These are lifestyle changes. I can think of no better way than to implement these practices into our routine until they become second nature to us. Then we are ready for whatever comes before us.

Personal Journal Notes

_____

_____

_____

_____

_____

_____

_____

_____

_____

_____

_____

_____

_____

_____

_____

_____

Part 3

Cool Downs/Extras/Advanced

The 6th Way: Give

Love is not an emptiness longing to be filled—it is a fullness pressing to be released. It is the power, the creative energy of love, bristling with activity and very much in need of an outlet, a place to flow to and something to become.
~ J. Kennedy Shultz

You Are the Power

Giving is a powerful exercise that builds spiritual muscle. When we are young, we grow accustomed to being given to and taken care of. We are loved. It is a whole other level of maturity to realize that we were born to give love out to others. Asking ourselves what we can give to a situation opens us up to realizing that we have a part to play in the world. Below are some ways we can move into greater giving and more fulfilling participation in the world around us. Any one of them is a perfect place to start. Giving is a very special spiritual practice because it is an expression of our divine nature, which is love. We are hardwired for it. There are many ways we can express love. As we grow in our awareness of ourselves, getting more and more in touch with our inner being, we receive more ideas about how we can contribute to the life that we know.

Ancient wisdom tells us that we cannot out-give God—the more we give, the more we receive. That is the wisdom of the ages and more specifically, the Law of Giving and Receiving. In giving, we receive immediately because the very act feeds our souls and brings us alive.

At an event we hosted years ago, Neale Donald Walsh, author of the *Conversations with God* series, said, "It is always right to give" when asked about giving to the homeless. Having been on the streets himself at one point because of health issues which led to the loss of employment, he knew the difficulties people encounter and how difficult it is to overcome and rise above all of that.

Giving money is a form of expressing love. My parents were very generous with the church, considering their income and responsibilities. My three brothers, my sister and I each had weekly envelopes for giving so we could get into the practice. We enjoyed a nice home and good food not only because my father worked hard, but because of my parents' generosity with family, friends and neighbors. My parents did well for themselves, considering my father never had a college education.

When I visited a Lutheran church in Tanzania on a medical mission, I was pleasantly surprised to see the size of their offering baskets: they were large enough to hold tithes of their first crops. After the service, these crops were sold in the courtyard and the monies given in support of the church. It was eye opening to see people with so little dedicated and committed to sharing and working the Principle of Life.

I believe everyone wants to give. Everyone wants to participate in a bigger idea than just themselves, even if they don't know it yet. I started giving what I thought I could. One day, my cousin Walter looked over my shoulder to see the check I was writing to the center and told me I could do better. I can't say I liked hearing that, but I knew he was right. I could, and I did. It was something I had to grow into in my own way and in my own time. Every time I increased it from there, the flow came back to me with even more.

Soon I became a committed giver and shortly after that I graduated to tithing. I bit the bullet and have never gone back. Tithing is a great tool to stretch us in our giving and help us see how much we are capable of. I had no idea that I could give so much!(Typically, tithing means giving ten percent of what we bring in.) Tithing is like using training wheels on a bike. We keep them on for as long as we need them and then we keep going, increasing the percentages or amounts as we go. Last year my husband suggested we give even more. I am happy to report it proved to be a very successful year financially, and in many other ways as well. Tithing helps release us from being controlled by money, which automatically opens us up to a greater flow of not only money, but all good things.

I heard of a tither who said, "I want to make so much money that I live on ten percent and give the rest away." What a prosperity consciousness! I have found that the more I stretch in my giving, the more prosperity I enjoy, the bigger I feel and the more I realize how much I am contributing to our world. After all, it is our world too, and contributing to it gives us part ownership of it. It also helps us show our appreciation for all that we've been given. Knowing we are one with Life brings us such great joy; it keeps us in the flow of even more.

Volunteering is another way to express love that exercises our spiritual muscles and builds stamina. There are so many non-profit organizations that do tremendous work on a shoestring budget who depend on the kindness and generosity of their volunteers. There are mothers who could use a couple of hours away for peace of mind who would love some help with their children. Running errands for the elderly or those who can't leave home due to an illness is another. Listening and giving our time to others in this way is probably the most loving act we can do for each other. Sharing our expertise is another resource we can give.

Giving of our time, talent and treasure is a great way to exercise our spiritual muscles and feel more expansion in our consciousness, which can only lead to bigger and more productive lives. Giving is an investment in ourselves and those around us. We all receive inspiration from those who are generous in the world. It helps us want to give more, too. This kind of example gives us ideas on how we can become a greater participant in life and help create a world that works for all. Giving is love. Love feeds our souls and strengthens us like nothing else can. We need it not only to survive, but to thrive.

Do I generously give of my time, energy, love and resources?

_____

What can I do to increase giving to myself? To others?

_____

_____

_____

_____

Personal Journal Notes

_____

_____

_____

_____

_____

_____

_____

_____

_____

_____

_____

_____

_____

_____

_____

The 7th Way: Rest & Flow

You do not need to leave your room. Remain sitting at your table and listen. Do not even listen, simply wait. Do not even wait, be quite still and solitary. The world will freely offer itself to you to be unmasked, it has no choice, it will roll in ecstasy at your feet.

~ Franz Kafka

Don't worry about what the world needs. Ask what makes you come alive and do that. Because what the world needs are people who have come alive.

~ Howard Thurman

There are times when it is important to our mental health and well-being to have some down time, to allow ourselves to just *be*. It's important to allow ourselves opportunities to do nothing. Filling ourselves back up or refueling is essential to our success and happiness.

Through Esther Hicks, the teaching of Abraham says we need rest, relaxation, time away, doodling... sometimes even staring at the walls. Everything serves.

Sound unproductive? It's not, really. Hard to believe some of us need permission for that kind of thing? It's true, some of us have been so programmed to *do*, be active and keep going that it is hard for us to believe that just *being* can be just as productive, and even more so.

Overworking seven days a week depletes our resources and stops the flow of creativity. Our lives are supposed to be balanced and harmonious at home and at work. Regular off time with no agenda, working in the garden, fishing, enjoying a hobby, reading, doing something fun, playing with children, spending leisurely time with our partner and time alone all serve us more than we know. There is a reason the seventh day of creation in the Creation story was designated a day of rest!

129

I used to work hard for months at a time and when I took a day off, I would get sick. I would overdo it, thinking it had to be that way and when I finally created an opening to relax, my body would collapse. I paid a price for not taking better care of myself all along. This can be avoided with regularly scheduled time off. It is critical to our health and well-being and greatly serves those around us as well. If we are happy, they are happier too. Time away can benefit us even more by giving us a new perspective. Sometimes we need to get away to appreciate what we have.

Am I kind to myself? _____

Do I allow myself time to do nothing? _____

Being Time

After my mother's memorial service, I remember sitting alone in my hotel room in downtown Milwaukee. This was the second of three memorial services held in her honor. One was in Columbia, South Carolina, where she lived; another was in Milwaukee, where she spent most of her adult life raising us; and the third was in St. Louis, where she grew up.

My husband and young son had stayed home for this one. My siblings and their partners were in their rooms. I remember staring at the blank wall, feeling such love after connecting with the many people who also cherished my mother. I thought about all the wonderful memories we shared together.

Due to my mother's type of illness we had three years to prepare for our final goodbye. We each gave her everything we could. My gracious husband took over our business and the care of our young son and our home so I could spend weeks away, being with her as much as possible. I felt good about our relationship, knowing we were complete. Knowing she was free was a true celebration. Feeling her freedom freed me up as well. I don't know what I saw on the wall, but there seemed to be an opening with love pouring out, and I was basking in it. I felt a love I had never felt before. All I needed to do was *be* and soak it in.

We have been offered the opportunity to live a great adventure with Life. We wouldn't be here if we hadn't said yes. What if we lived each moment and day full of excitement and enthusiasm for the gift we have been given? How much more fun it could be!

When someone makes us an offer we can't refuse, we jump at it. We recognize a good thing when we see it. The things we thought were so important to us before are pushed aside for the new, exciting possibility that lies before us. We are there. Count us in. There is no hesitation. We do whatever needs to be done so we can move into the new experience. We would be fools not to. The same is true with Life. Every day we are given an outstanding, exceptional chance to be alive and experience a deeper, richer life. We can accept the offer that Life continues to extend and enjoy the perfection of it all right where we are. All we have to do is say yes.

> *When a Great Adventure is offered, you don't refuse it.*
> ~ Amelia Earhart

Do I allow myself time to soak in whatever is happening and be with myself and my feelings? _____

Do I schedule time and space for a date with myself?

_____

What could I do differently to give myself time to just Be?

_____
_____
_____
_____
_____
_____

Living in the Flow

Life is not meant to be hard work, challenging us to do things that do not feel loving or expressions of our gift. Everyday miracles become the most natural part of our lives when we give Life all we have and follow IT's lead.

Years ago, our administrative assistant, Stacey, wasn't sure how she could afford to continue going to school. She loved the Nature Center and spent hours helping there while attending a prestigious private college in an exclusive area just outside of Orlando. One day she received a community service grant which allowed her to work on her master's degree. As one can imagine, we were all elated to hear about her gift. A stipulation of the grant required her to give a number of hours every year to the Nature Center. In return for doing what she already loved to do, her education would be paid for. The fruits of her labor became evident. For the fun of it, I asked if she could put a dollar amount on that grant. She estimated it to be worth about $22,000! That's quite a sum! Some people work all year long for a salary like that. Her generosity with the Nature Center paid off. Givers must be taken care of, and Life will find a way. That's *living in the flow*.

Sitting back and soaking in the immensity of her demonstration felt so good not only to her, but also to all of those who observed this beautiful miracle.

When we:

- make a commitment to a higher idea
- hold a vision for ourselves that is positive and inspiring
- know the Universal Truth Principles and how Life works
- circulate our good
- forgive the past
- live in gratitude and appreciation

We are in the flow.

We don't have to do anything. We are exactly where we need to be. We live in the flow when we give up strain or struggle; when we stop trying to make things happen. Life is much easier when we live it the way it was designed to be lived.

How do I live in the flow?

_____

_____

_____

_____

Mini Sabbatical

At one point we rented space downtown from a non-profit organization. The founder had returned from being away for two weeks at a conference. Her mini sabbatical helped her see that she had been spreading herself too thin, caught up in too many of the details of being an entrepreneur. Time away allowed her to get in touch with her feelings. She had lost touch with who she was and what she was doing. Now she was able to see what was most important to her.

She decided to focus on those things that inspired her, like teaching and writing, and delegate the organizational jobs to the others who were good at them. The shift in paradigm made a huge difference in defining what was hers to do and what was not. She could have continued for quite awhile in the same old way but would have been unhappy. Instead she was renewed and inspired, and it made all the difference. Things work for us when we get ourselves into a better place.

Living in the flow is a *cool down exercise,* allowing ourselves to be, taking time out tore-evaluate our life, our work...taking time to reassess where we are and where we want to be...maybe even *who* we are and *who* we want to be.

Do I schedule time away to get refreshed so I can renew my perspective? _____

Do I take time to evaluate my life? _____

How could I arrange to find that kind of time?

_____

_____

_____

_____

_____

_____

Kayaking the Russian River

On one summer vacation our family kayaked down the Russian River through the wine country of northern California. It was a gorgeous setting and an amazing day we will always remember. The only time we used our oars was to move faster or keep us from running into trees and bushes along the water's edge. Other than that, we were carried downstream by the powerful flow of the river.

Near the end of our trip our guide found the perfect place for us to go for a swim. It was a hot summer day, and we had been active! We had bicycled through vineyards, lunched outside one of the wineries, and then kayaked down the river. At that point it didn't take much convincing to get us to jump in for a swim to cool off. The water was so clear and refreshing - what a ride it was!

All we had to do was just float in the water and the river carried us with it. It felt so good. Of course, wading upstream was a different matter altogether. Big difference between going with the flow and going against it!

The experience reminded me that Life is like the river. It, too, will take us with it as long as we don't interfere—which we often do. As long as we don't want something that is upstream, we are automatically moving in the right direction. How much of our lives do we spend wanting something upstream when all the goods really are downstream? Life is meant to be easy.

What benefits do I see from floating downstream versus paddling upstream in my life?

1. _____
2. _____
3. _____
4. _____
5. _____
6. _____

Mantras and Babies

When our son Joseph was about 3, he became very impatient whenever we were stopped at a red light. It didn't matter that there were cars in front of us, he wanted to keep going! He enjoyed moving and could only think about going forward.

There was nothing I could do about the traffic, but there had to be something I could do to distract him and keep him from losing his cool in the back seat. After all, stoplights are a part of life as we know it. He was going to have to get used to them one way or another.

The idea came to me to start the mantra, "We're in the Flow." Over and over again we would yell out the phrase. Interestingly, whenever we both took it on, traffic moved. I don't know if it really had anything to do with getting things going or not. I do know the mantra helped him feel like there was something he could do about the situation, and it gave me peace of mind while driving, which helped us both. I still use it today whenever I am in a hurry and traffic seems congested. Not surprisingly, it always works.

I also use that idea today whenever I want to remind myself that my consciousness can make a difference wherever I am. Flow is our natural state of being. In Life, we are always in the flow to the degree that we recognize that we are.

A friend once said, "When Momma is happy, everyone is happy!" I believe that applies to us all. Taking care of ourselves affects everything we do and those around us. When our energy is low, it's an indicator that it is time to retreat. We get into trouble by not having our wits about us and doing something crazy. As we learn to better love and care for ourselves by taking the time we need to replenish, *everyone* around us reaps the benefits of our being in a good place. We all are blessed by seeing happy people.

What changes do I need to make to increase my flow?

_____

_____

_____

_____

_____

_____

What action steps would open me up to greater flow in my life?

1. _____
2. _____
3. _____
4. _____
5. _____
6. _____

Our assistant, Stacey, was living in the flow as she continued to move forward and followed her inner guidance to apply for a grant that would allow her to continue her education. Our landlady was living in the flow when she said yes to getting away, taking time out by herself, and exposing herself to new, uplifting ideas... receiving new direction and once again loving what she does. Joseph and I were living in the flow in traffic as soon as we got into alignment with a greater idea. Thoroughly enjoying our family outing while floating down the Russian River felt luxuriously like flow. In a friendly universe we can choose to live together in the flow and see what more Life has in store for us. It can only be good!

Finding ways to celebrate and appreciate ourselves, our growth and expansion, who we have become, and the others around us is an essential way to exercise our spiritual muscles. Observing and appreciating all the love and goodness we have fills us up and gives us the impetus we need to keep going and see how much more life has in store for us.

Personal Journal Notes

_____

_____

_____

_____

_____

_____

_____

_____

_____

_____

_____

_____

_____

_____

_____

_____

_____

Advanced Spiritual Workouts

It is never too late to be what you might have become.
~ George Eliot

If you really want to help this world, what you have to teach is how to live in it. And that no one can do who has not himself learned how to live in it in the joyful sorrow and the sorrowful joy of the knowledge of life as it is.
~ Joseph Campbell

Sacred Covenant

In my early days of ministry, I went nonstop. Even with loads of help – like a good husband, an assistant minster who also served as our executive director and dear friend, and a cleaning service that came every other week – there were lots of demands that came with being the senior minister, being actively involved with my older two children, and having a new baby. Looking back, I don't know how I did it! In my spiritual work I went for it all, and it all showed up. I said I was ready to get back in the game after being out of it for a while. I loved being back in it! My life was rich and full like nothing I had ever experienced before. I just had to find a way to keep up.

As much as I was teaching and experiencing great results from my work, I would wake up some mornings and forget what was for me to do and what was the Universe's to do. I kept falling into the trap of trying to do everything myself, leaving me confused, frustrated and worn out. I hadn't fully worked it out in my mind that I had an infinite partner that is available 24/7.

I realized my time was too precious to be doing more than I needed, so I came up with the idea of a sacred covenant that would specifically define what my part was and what was the Universe's. What a relief that was to me! Here was something I could review before getting out of bed in the morning that helped me remember what was for me to do. No, I didn't have to make anything happen. I just had to know that all was taken care of.

What is a sacred covenant? *A sacred covenant is a finely tuned agreement created between ourselves and the Infinite.* It is updated and changed along the way as we gain greater clarity. It could even be called a sacred agreement, if that sounds better. This is what we live by. These are the rules of our life. They help us stay on track.

Charles and Myrtle Fillmore, the founders of Unity, created a beautiful covenant with God. In exchange for being taken care of and supported by the Infinite, they agreed to dedicate their lives to their work and to helping people live greatly. What a concept!

The covenant also clarifies what is ours to do and what is God's. It helps us remember that we don't have to hold the world together on our own. We were never meant to do life alone. Working on our partnership with Spirit, with Life, strengthens our spiritual muscles and gives us the confidence we need to live boldly and beautifully. There are a lot of things already in place with which we don't have to concern ourselves. When we get a grasp on what those are, we can release the pressure and free ourselves up for more of what we want.

A sacred covenant can bring us great peace of mind about life. Once we get it down and know it well, we carry it with us in our heart to draw upon whenever we need or want. It is a beautiful spiritual practice.

It's another tool in the toolbox, helping us to keep things straight in our head. What is our part? What are we committing to? What's the gift already given? What is already in place that we never have to worry about? That's the Universe's part.

Are we telling God what to do? It does sound like a bold thing to do, doesn't it? Here's an example of what the Universe agrees to do:

- Love and support us
- Orchestrate our life
- Divinely place us and our family in the right and perfect place where we can experience the greatest ease, prosperity and joy

In truth, all these things are a given, but are *we* clear about that? Do we really *know* it? This part of the agreement was more for me than it was for Spirit. Getting myself into alignment with what I knew to be true made it easy for me to relax and follow Spirit's lead. After all, I work for the Universe. The rest was and continues to be taken care of on my and everyone else's behalf.

By defining in our own words how *we* receive that support and love, we can attract the kind of care that is more specific to our needs and desires. Personalizing and clarifying the picture of what we want to experience invites outcomes that are most ideal for us. This spiritual exercise helps us remember our agreement and move into our day from a more powerful place.

We may say we know these basic concepts, but do we really have them fully integrated into our entire being? We may not know them at all, and that makes things even more difficult. Even if we *do* understand these concepts, it is easy to get distracted and forget the Truth.

Reviewing these points every day (preferably before getting out of bed and starting the day, especially when we have to hit the ground running) gets us into the routine until it becomes a habit. Even then we may want to revisit them from time to time. Muscle memory is important in physical exercise, and it's no different for our spiritual well-being. This practice really made a difference in making my life manageable and helped me stay true to my soul by relaxing and trusting in Spirit.

Ready for greater ease, support and fun? I know I am! Here's the basic format:

> Why am I here? *I AM HERE TO...*
> I AM statements or affirmations: *I AM...*
> Daily agreements & commitments: *I AGREE TO...*
> Recognition of Truth: *THE UNIVERSE AGREES TO...*
> Gratitude statement: *I AM GRATEFUL FOR...*
> Dedications: *I DEDICATE MY LIFE TO...*
> Honoring the process: *THE UNIVERSE DEDICATES ITS LIFE TO...*
> Closing: *AND SO IT IS!*

A full-page version of the Sacred Covenant form is also included at the back of this workbook for you to copy and use daily.

Below is an example of my personal covenant with Spirit. **I highly suggest writing something regarding your own covenant before you read it**, so that you won't be influenced by what I wrote. This practice will be much more effective and beneficial if it is tailored to each person and how they see fit. Listening with our heart and utilizing a language that speaks to us will create the ideal covenant for each of us.

My Sacred Covenant:

I AM HERE TO: *I am here to experience more God; to experience myself as God; to support others in experiencing more God, experiencing themselves as God and in supporting others to do the same.*

I AM: *I am a clear, practical teacher of the Truth. I am a powerful voice for God.*

I AGREE TO: *I agree to be the fullest expression of Spirit I came here to be; to come from the highest, most loving and abundant consciousness at all times; to love, respect and value myself, my life and my work, and to love, respect and value others, their lives and their work; to see the perfection of God in everyone and everything, especially in myself and my family; and to bring my best love and attention to everyone and everything this day and every day.*

THE UNIVERSE AGREES TO: *The Universe agrees to love and support us; to orchestrate our lives; to divinely place me and my family in the right and perfect situations where we experience the greatest ease, prosperity and joy.*

I AM GRATEFUL FOR: *I am grateful for our ever-deepening, expanding partnership together.*

I DEDICATE MY LIFE TO: *I dedicate my life to the one Life we are all living together.*

THE UNIVERSE DEDICATES ITS LIFE TO: *The Universe dedicates ITs Life to helping us realize that we are already free.*

...AND SO IT IS!

Sacred-Space Covenant

If we believe that Good (or God) is infinite (which means everywhere), then every place is sacred space—not just a church or a shrine—*everywhere*, all at the same time. Sometimes it is helpful to recognize and remember just how special it is right where we are. It's hard to believe that all of God is present at every point of existence, which means right where I am and right where you are. No matter how dark or dreary a place may be physically or mentally, it is empowering to remember we are standing on sacred ground and always immersed in Spirit.

By consciously focusing on the Presence and Power that we live in and are immersed in, we can create our own special places that remind us of this reality and support the harmony and balance we need in our homes, our workplaces and everywhere we come together with others. These spaces are not necessarily physical spaces, but they can be. Most of all, setting the consciousness of what we desire to see puts in motion a greater dynamic. We can accomplish great things when we first create a safe, sacred place in our minds where we can be ourselves and express openly.

The idea of a Sacred-Space Covenant came years ago when I was teaching an upper level ministerial class for the first time. A student admitted she did not feel safe to speak and share. I myself was challenged by some strong personalities in the class who were convinced *they* had all the answers. I was also younger than many of them, which may have added to my intimidation. It was uncomfortable for us all. I was so grateful that this woman (who just so happened to be a therapist) spoke up. When we talked privately, she shared some ideas. Together we worked on a way to take control of the mental space we shared in class and make it conducive to higher learning for us all.

This is what we came up with: Create a covenant whereby everyone was expected to respect one another's perspectives and stay on the same page. It made all the difference.

We started out with a Mind Treatment to accompany our covenant:

I live in a universe that welcomes me just as I am. God created me as a perfect expression of ITself and accepts me with unconditional love ad provides me with the space I need to live comfortably and easily. I know this sacred space is essential to my well-being. It frees me to accept my humanness, my imperfections, and more and more to appreciate my divine nature.

I freely and lovingly make this kind of space available to others who are near me, allowing them to be their real, true selves. I extend my heart, I provide the wisdom available to me when asked, and choose words which neither impose nor judge, but guide others in knowing what is right for them. I am divinely supported in knowing how to do this.

I give thanks for knowing sacred space is provided for us all. I enjoy living in a universe of Love. And so it is!

Our Sacred-Space Covenant:
   I agree to listen and be present, and not try to fix or give advice.
   I agree to bring my best love and attention to whatever or whomever is before me, including—and especially—myself.
   I agree to practice non-judgment.
   I agree to love and accept myself and others as they are.
   I agree to stay in the present, the Now moment of Power.
   I use as my guide: If it is loving, if it grows, expands or deepens love, it's the right thing to do!
   Signed _____
   Date _____

This covenant may be used as a guide to create your own sacred mental spaces. There may already be special places or groups of people that nurture your spirit, and there may be some other situations that need healthy, loving structure. Creating a sacred space covenant could provide the guidelines needed to uplift the consciousness of those participating, taking all to a new level. A form for creating a Sacred-Space Covenant is also included in the back of this workbook.

Timeline

The purpose of a timeline is to get to know ourselves better and to review where we are in life. For the most part we don't take the time to reflect on what has happened and how it led us to where we are now, often causing us to repeat the past. We aren't meant to dwell on the past, but it is interesting to see how the puzzle pieces of our lives come together. Life builds on itself. Growth is incremental. It's important to appreciate all the good that led up to where we are now...to see the progression...the evolution of consciousness. Sometimes we need to take a reading to see where that might be, how far we have come, and what we need to work on next.

Creating a timeline is a fun exercise to do with a partner or as part of a class or group of friends. Working and sharing together gives us ideas that we may not think of on our own. Doing this exercise together helps us build on what others are doing. It's a beautiful thing to see the group mind at work and how individual input dovetails with others and their situations. It makes it easier to look at some of the difficult things we face as humans and learn that we are not alone in our experiences. Sharing with others how we worked through challenging situations or navigated new territories benefits us all. Building a timeline is worthwhile, whether we do it alone or with others.

This exercise gives us:

- Personal attention
- A different perspective on our life
- Answers we need
- Appreciation for who we are and where we came from
- The opportunity to see the good that may have been hidden
- A greater understanding about Life and how we can work with It.

That's the goal.

When I turned 30, my whole life fell apart. While it looked like a perfect setup from the outside, the foundation of my life and my marriage was built on sand. Not much stability there. I was too young to question the health of our relationship and the life we had created. I was too naïve to see serious problems on the horizon and what that would mean not only to me, but to my husband, our children, our families and all those who were close to us.

Leading up to our demise, my firefighter father died in a fire but was brought back to life and went into coma (which lasted 13 years). While my husband was traveling for weeks at a time with Secret Service details during an election year, I was alone at home with our two young children in a new city. The list goes on and on. It was a disaster! After that crash and burn, I had to find myself all over again. I wandered in a mental, emotional and spiritual desert, not knowing which way to turn. I found the Science of Mind teaching through Walter, an older cousin of mine, whom I have always respected. He highly recommended that I give this new spiritual center a try. It was there that I found life. It was like I had just come home for the first time. I found others who had experienced the very same feeling that I did. I was surrounded by people who wanted more for themselves, who were working on letting go of the past and learning how to love and forgive themselves. Here we were all given an opportunity to create a new life built on spiritually substantial footings that could withstand our new, robust way of living.

Decades later, I can see what a blessing it was to have a second chance at life. Because learning and growing are ongoing processes for us all, there will always be more for us to expand into and become. Life was designed to improve for us as we go. Throughout our lives we have opportunities to meet up with our past. If we have significantly grown mentally, emotionally and spiritually, we may be able to see it from a new perspective.

I had one such experience that enlightened me. One January I decided to visit my daughter in Wisconsin. Yes, it was a crazy time of year to go, but believe it or not, I missed the cold and snow after living in the southeast part of the U.S. for 30 years. I hadn't been back for a very long time because Liz usually comes to the Orlando area for some sun and warmth. It was a real treat to take walks outside in the cold with snow falling all around.

During that visit I also had opportunities to see my past as I always remembered it and to choose to see it with fresh eyes, from the perspective of where I am now. I had hoped to have some quiet time to write while my daughter was busy at work and be with her when she was off. However, during my stay there was a death in the family, which put me in contact with extended family with whom I had been out of touch for a long time.

My godfather (who was an older cousin of mine) had passed away. Circumstances made it too difficult for me to attend his memorial service, which was still a couple of hours away. I did have an opportunity to talk to his sister(who was also my cousin) and give my condolences by phone. We were able to share some wonderful things together that we may not have discussed had we been in the company of others.

She told me how important my mother was to the family, and that she had been a light and brought a youthfulness and creativity that was refreshing to them. What she shared helped me to see my mother in a new way. I also saw myself in a new way. Memories of growing up in the area surfaced. It was easy to see I was no longer the same person. In fact, I had grown and changed tremendously. It helped me appreciate who I am today. It's important to acknowledge how far we've come and that we've moved on in our lives. We are not the same as we were.

Because we get a larger, more inclusive view of what transpired, our timelines give us a larger view of ourselves, a plan, something we haven't heard of before, and even the possibility of a new direction. We begin to see the real masterpiece that is underway. It's easy to get caught up in the details of our lives. When we rarely take time to step back and see the bigger picture, we can miss so much. Amazing and incredible things happen all the time that we miss when we are focused on the details and not the bigger picture. There are dots to be connected in order to see what we just couldn't see before. This helps us to have an appreciation for Life and to see how IT is always looking out for us and seeking expansion in, around and through us. Things have always been and continue to happen right under our noses. There is more to life than meets the eye.

The Universe has the biggest possible picture for us. IT knows our potential. I'm not saying we don't have a say in what goes on. It's just that the greater Mind—that created us in the first place as part of ITself—holds the intention set for us from the very beginning of our creation for the greatest possible outcome for us. That's not something we can do. Our Creator knows us better than we know ourselves. IT has an agenda for us to evolve and experience more freedom, more prosperity, more joy and more health and well-being. Why *wouldn't* our Source want those things for us? Especially because IT is us. God wants to experience ITself as all of this. There's much to see when we take our blinders off. We can begin to see that we are a part of a magnificent universe.

Staying connected to the unfolding of the bigger picture makes a difference in the kind of life we will live. Suddenly our existence has much more meaning because we can see that each little move, every single advance, takes us into the realization of something even greater. Looking at things with new eyes helps us understand why we are so frustrated with limitation and small-mindedness. We were created for more. There's no settling for less and being happy. We have a desire to move into a life that matters and fulfills a greater purpose. Mundane things that we used to dread now become fascinating, and we are eager to participate in them because there is a compelling reason behind our doing them. They make us feel alive where they didn't before because they appeared to be isolated events that had to be taken care of...routines, ruts or mere tasks we looked upon with disdain that kept us from doing what we wanted.

Staying connected to a more expansive and engaging picture keeps us from getting distracted by small, unnecessary details and keeps us focused on what is real. That is why it is important that we take our time with this exercise. We can work on it for a bit and then let it simmer on the back burner, allowing other memories to come forward so a greater truth can be revealed.

It helps us to take time to get to know ourselves. What is the part of us that helped make all of this happen? What is the part of us that is unaffected by all that has gone on? That is strong and resilient? We may want to journal about this to help facilitate even more information or intelligence that wants to be known. Some people love to journal, while others want nothing to do with it. I like to suggest it because it is the fastest way I know to get things out of our heads and free up precious mind space for other things. New ideas and thoughts need to be put down on paper. In our busy days we may think we have grasped a brilliant idea that we are convinced we will never forget. We may even have a vision of what is possible and think that we've got it forever. We now understand the meaning of Life! Yet the next day we are sidetracked with other conditions demanding our attention and we totally forget what we were so sure we would remember forever. When we write it down, we have something we can go back to the next day or years later and be reminded of the awesome thing that happened for us, reactivating our state of appreciation. We can use that as a base from which to jump to even greater visions of what is possible. One glimpse can build on another until we really have quite an exquisite, breathtaking picture. That is what makes living worthwhile!

We begin to see some continuity as we go...how often great and even extraordinary things have happened to us. It becomes clear how responsive the Universe really is to us when we remember asking for something one day and immediately things began to shift. Entries don't have to be big, long dissertations. Notes can be shorthand, pictures, diagrams or whatever we can look back at and understand. It's totally personal. No one else needs to see it or understand what means so much.

A good resource for ideas is the book *How to Think like Leonardo da Vinci: 7 Steps to Genius Every Day,* by Michael J. Gelb. We don't have to be scientists, artists or experts to have permission to create something wonderful and meaningful to us.

How do we make our timelines? That's entirely an individual choice. This is where our creativity comes into play. It can be a straight horizontal line across a poster board, large sticky note or loose-leaf paper, with chronologically important years or estimates placed vertically along it. Keep in mind this masterpiece will need to be safely stored, possibly for years, so size could be an issue. Poster board can be bought in smaller sizes or folded if necessary. This project can be done in a creative, colorful and fun way that is meaningful to each person. We can start by writing what comes to mind and then review our intention.

One method is to make a flow chart of what we want to include and later make it permanent when we are sure it contains everything we want (many of us come up with even more ideas as we go). Another option is to do a detailed biography with pictures and reframe them with our current outlook. Collages or putting pictures with words is another way to express ourselves.

To start a timeline, draw a horizontal line across a page and insert key dates beginning with the year you were born. You can also include:

- Key events
- Important people
- Drastic changes
- "Aha" moments you will never forget because they really made a difference for you
- Growth
- Moves
- Upsets
- Plans that were changed (you were supposed to go to one school but ended up at different one; you were supposed to go out with one person but ended up with someone else...how that changed things and turned the course of your life forever)

These are the kinds of things we want to document.

There are many options. It's up to us what we want to include and what is important to us. We don't necessarily have to include our 16th birthday, but we do want to include life-changing events. It's an individual preference as to how deep we go with this, how detailed we want to get with our descriptions, and how close to the heart we feel we can go. Take note of any feelings or emotions that are triggered by the past that may need some extra attention. Remember and use the *Ho'oponopono* prayer for something we can do to bring immediate relief. If our emotions become particularly bothersome, we may need professional help facing them so we can be free of whatever hold they have on us. Uncomfortable feelings or blocks are deeper levels of peeling the onion and may be what's getting in our way.

We need not worry about anyone else seeing this – unless, of course, we want to share it with others. This is for our eyes only. We can think about it deeply or not. That depends on the individual. This is something we may want to add to months or years later whenever a new awareness, perception or insight comes to mind that would be worth documenting. It could be kept in a special folder where we might keep spiritual projects and exercises that we are working on. Instead of doing it as an assignment and moving through it as fast as we can, it's important to take the time to savor the process. The more time we focus on it, the more we will get out of it. Each life is unique! Everyone has gems that have been hidden and need to be uncovered or rediscovered from a new vantage point.

Again, this is for our eyes only and may open our awareness to some personal work that still needs to be done. That's part of it. We all have areas that are underdeveloped and still in need of work. We are all "in process." That's a good thing!

Timeline Questions

Making a timeline presents an opportunity to think about our life. Focusing on a key event, consider:

What was I going through at the time and how did I feel about it?

_____
_____
_____
_____

How did I resolve or get over a life challenge?

_____
_____
_____
_____

Is there a pattern in my life that becomes clear?

_____
_____
_____
_____

What key events influenced my life?
1. _____
2. _____
3. _____

    4. _____

    5. _____

Who were some of the important people in my life?

    1. _____

    2. _____

    3. _____

    4. _____

    5. _____

What gifts did they give me?

    1. _____

    2. _____

    3. _____

    4. _____

    5. _____

What drastic or upsetting changes took place in my life?

_____

_____

_____

_____

What moments were eye openers that I will never forget?

_____

_____

_____

_____

What experiences really caused me to grow?

_____

_____

_____

_____

What moves did I make in my life and how did they change me?

_____

_____

What upsets took place that were unexpected?

What plans or changes took place that were "supposed" to happen?

This might be interesting for others to find after we are gone. Even the challenges or incomplete parts may touch those close to us and help them to see us as relatable. Maybe our loved ones are going through similar difficulties and/or milestone occasions to celebrate.

Extra Timeline Challenge

In his classic, *The 7 Habits of Highly Effective People*, Rev. Stephen Covey instructs us to "begin with the end in mind." He suggests that we pretend that we are going to a memorial service, and as we look around, we discover it is our very own. The question is, what are people saying about us? What would we like for them to say about us? For what would we like to be respected or admired? What qualities? How have we made a difference? How will we be remembered?

It's a bold invitation. Most of us have not gone there before. It can be fun and exciting, especially after making peace with the idea that we will not live in this physical form forever. Sooner or later we all will transition. This exercise is less about what others will think of us when we are gone and more about getting to know ourselves better and seeing what we value. It may also show us areas we need to improve and give further attention.

In doing this exercise, some people have moved from the chronological timeline to events and experiences, and then on to concepts in their lives and when they were introduced. They created an intangible timeline which proved to be even more enlightening.

It's our choice how far we want to take this. If it has energy to it, it's best to keep going. Rarely do we give ourselves permission to look further into our true selves. If it feeds us, it's a good sign that the exercise is being effective.

There is no right or wrong way to do this. We can draw out any buried treasures that we find and take them with us on our path. In our busyness we often forget what happened yesterday. Taking time to appreciate synchronicities and connections makes all the difference. To some, this exercise may feel like play or make them curious and see wonderful things that have happened. Others may feel differently and that's okay, too!

What are people saying about me at the end of my life?

_____

_____

_____

_____

What would I like them to say?

_____

_____

_____

_____

What qualities would I like to be respected for?

_____

_____

_____

_____

What qualities would I like to be admired for?

_____

_____

_____

_____

How have I made a difference?

_____
_____
_____
_____

What did I accomplish that I am proud of?

_____
_____
_____
_____

How will I be remembered?

_____
_____
_____
_____

One Step Further

New Thought teacher Rev. Mary Morrissey, creator of the "Prosperity Plus" programs, suggests that we take this step. It is even more bold – to consider a date for our end of life. How do we want to feel then? Whom do we want in our life? How do we want this to look? How do we want this to go down before we leave? Don't worry, because there is plenty of time to change that date as we go and fill up our lives with even more good stuff!

This is a very courageous endeavor. Not everyone is ready to go there. Some of us are, others are not. I am throwing it out there for those who are.

Can I consider a date for the end of my life? _____

If so, what would it be? _____

How would I want to feel then?

_____
_____

_____

_____

How do I want the end of my life to look?

_____

_____

_____

_____

Whom do I want to be there with me?

_____

_____

_____

_____

What would I need to have happen to feel complete with this life?

_____

_____

_____

_____

End-of-Life Challenge Takers

The end-of-life challenge was illuminating for me. Of course, I wanted people to think well of me... that I was kind and compassionate. When I thought more about it, I realized that is all tied to ego. We want people to think well of us. I thought, what if they thought she really wouldn't have cared what we were thinking right now. She did what she wanted to do. Hoping that what I wanted to do was done in the spirit of kindness and love.

~ Marie B.

When I did my end of life challenge, the thing that came up for me was that I didn't care what other people thought of me. I was listing things I wanted to accomplish. It was interesting. I was going to have two husbands while living to 120. And there was one husband that I was focusing on. Looking back, it was what I really would like.

~ Libby F.

One of the things that inspired me about being in my 90s was that I read an article about a man who built ships, and another about a woman running marathons. Both were in their 90s. I thought, I want to be doing what I love and be healthy until I make my transition.

~ Mike L.

I always think about people in my life who have passed and how they have affected me...how they made me feel. What I hope people would say about me is that I impacted their lives to help them find themselves, inspire them in some way, give them back to themselves somehow...that I might have had that effect on their lives.

~ Evelyn T.

I would want people to say she did what she could; she did her best and lived [her life] well.

~ Lydia M.

I kind of came to the end of life thing abruptly. I was going to the doctor's office and having blood work done. They said, we have a new test and we want to check this out. It shows how your body systems are doing on the inside (high tech). The one thing that it showed was that I have the highest stress level they had ever tested. This is not a good thing, because I want to live to be 110. It makes me wonder if, truly wonder, if my job is worth the stress.

~ Phillip D.

To help us get more comfortable with this conversation, I recall this magnificent piece by one of my favorites, Elizabeth Kübler-Ross, a medical doctor and pioneer whose work focused on death and dying. Here she shares her deepest understanding of what is most important in life:

Unconditional Love

Look forward to your transition.

It's the first time you will experience unconditional love.

There will be all peace and love, and all the nightmares and the turmoil you went through in your life will be like nothing.

When you make your transition, you are asked two things, basically:

How much love you have been able to give and receive,

and how much service you have rendered.

And you will know every consequence of every deed, every thought,

and every word you have ever uttered.

And that is, symbolically speaking, going through hell

when you see how many chances you missed.

But you also see how a nice act of kindness

has touched hundreds of lives that you're totally unaware of.

So concentrate on love while you're still around,

and teach your children early unconditional love.

So remember, concentrate on love, and look forward to the transition.

It's the most beautiful experience you can ever imagine.

Vayas con Dios!

~ Elizabeth Kübler-Ross

The timeline is a great thing to look at from time to time. One student shared,

When I first looked at my past, I saw so much healing had taken place. I thought how much more could I gain from reviewing? Then, the thought came to me that there is no limit to love and it's never going to run out. I thought I could look at it again because I would see it with fresh, new eyes. This gave me a chance to feel more and do the Ho'oponopono exercise [Chapter 7]. Looking at it again gave me more clarity about what has been in my life and made it all more fun. It cleared away any residual, old energy and allowed new energy to come in.

The work we do on our timelines helps us make the connections we want to see for our next advanced spiritual exercise: spiritual autobiographies. In doing this, we get to focus on ourselves in a different way so we can learn even more. These exercises are great ways to take time to love ourselves, give ourselves permission to be real and appreciate the fabulous beings that we are. Some loving kindness and forgiveness may also be required.

Spiritual Autobiography

Spiritual autobiographies dovetail beautifully with timelines. The autobiography takes things further by allowing us to see the deeper reasons why things are the way they are. They can be done as a solo project, or they can build on the work we did on our timelines.

When we look with eyes of love at what has been, we will see things we weren't able to notice before and appreciate how perfectly the divine hand of Life was at work all along. Our spiritual autobiography gives us a long-range perspective, more of the real story than just events. We have a chance to appreciate our very own spiritual awakening and see how perfectly things unfolded to support us in being all we came here to be. It's easy to forget how much love and support there really was along the way, even if it was only a vague sense of belonging to Life. Life loves all of ITs creations immensely, but we may not always be able to see or feel that love, depending on where we are.

When we really look, it's amazing what we find. This is a great exercise to help us appreciate all the gifts we have been given. It's surprising to see how many there really are. Even though there are things we might like to forget, we may be able to see these incidents in a new light from where we stand now. This helps set the stage for future work. It's a great place to start. When we see Infinite Intelligence has been at work all along, it will help us to trust that we are always in divine hands, always have been, and that our future will proceed with the same guarantee. *Somehow, I have been taken care of all these years that I have lived. Whatever makes me doubt that I won't also be provided for through the exit door?*

In the biography *Ernest Holmes, His Life and Times,* Fenwick (his brother) recalled, "Mom always took us to free places-- we spent long hours in the library, playing in public parks, walking here and there... discovering so much. We enjoyed feeling and being abundant and free."

They never knew their family was poor. Going through this process can help us re-evaluate our past and appreciate more of it. Clearing and cleaning old memories and perceptions opens us up to greater freedom and peace of mind. Looking at things with maturely developed and insightful eyes makes it possible for us to rewrite our history and convert the old into something inspiring and new.

The questions below will help organize our thoughts and give new perspectives to consider. Space is provided at the end of this section for answers:

- Who were the key players in my life?
- Who were the people who influenced my thinking and what I value today?
- What events, circumstances and situations happened that helped make me who I am today?
- Who were my teachers, my spiritual leaders and mentors, writers that touched me and helped me think and grow? Strangers that said something to me that I will never forget?
- How has my concept of God changed through the years? What was my first idea of God and how has it evolved over the years? What is it now? Where would I like it to be?
- What shifts took place in my thinking that turned things around for me? What gifts came out of the difficult years?
- What did I do that really made me happy?
- What has brought me to the point where I am now on my spiritual path?

Further questions to ask ourselves:

- What's calling me now?
- What am I going to find or what am I hoping to find when I answer that call?

As I discussed in Chapter 7 on Release, years ago I felt a strong call from the mountains. I longed for some time alone in a beautiful setting where I could focus on writing. One Friday morning during a weekly call with my prayer partner, a call came in. I checked the message later and it was from a very special woman who had once been a part of our community. As part of her studying and purposefully creating a new life for herself, she demonstrated a spectacular home near the top of a mountain outside of Waynesville, North Carolina. The voice mail was an invitation for me to use her place whenever she was away! I had just been saying, "I need a retreat. I need to get away!"

I jumped at the opportunity immediately. The serendipity of this invitation made it impossible for me to ignore. She planned to leave in a month. I couldn't wait to pack and head for the hills!

What happened when I arrived was much different from what I had imagined: I spent time dealing with some unresolved fears from the past. To begin with, it was February on the north face of the mountain. I didn't have a four-wheel drive vehicle, and it was questionable whether I could make it up the mountain without one. My friend had already left so I had to keep calling her neighbor to get a report on the weather and road conditions.

My intention was to finish my book, but I spent most of my time dealing with myself and some deep-seated fears. Although things happened in a much different way than I had envisioned, I received more than I could ever have asked for.

Finishing my book was not what the Universe had planned for me during this getaway. It was clear that bigger plans than mine were underway. This turned out to be yet another vision quest. It was a spiritual journey into myself. Being alone, I got to face who I was and all my fears. While I didn't finish my book, the experience itself gave me the perfect beginning to my book, which would never have happened had I not answered the mountains' call, or more importantly, Spirit's call. Once I realized all of that, I saw how exquisitely and divinely designed my experience was by the Infinite Creator of all, that knew exactly what I needed. Looking back, I would have to say this was an essential part of my spiritual path. It was a real turning point for me. Without it, I would not be where I am today.

Who were the key players in my life?

_____
_____
_____
_____

Who were the people who influenced my thinking and what I value today?

_____
_____
_____
_____

What events, circumstances and situations happened that helped make me who I am today?

_____
_____
_____
_____

Who were my teachers, my spiritual leaders and mentors, writers that touched me and helped me think and grow?

_____
_____
_____
_____

Who were the strangers that said something to me that I will never forget?

_____
_____
_____
_____

How has my concept of God changed through the years? What was my first idea of God and how has it evolved over the years?

_____
_____

_____
_____

What is it now?

_____
_____
_____
_____

What would I like it to be?

_____
_____
_____
_____

What shifts took place in my thinking that turned things around for me?

_____
_____
_____
_____

What gifts came out of the difficult years?

_____
_____
_____
_____

What did I do that really made me happy?

_____
_____
_____
_____

What has brought me to the point where I am now on my spiritual path?

_____
_____
_____

_____
_____
_____

Contemplating how we got to where we are today can be an inspiration or source of insights about where we might be headed, or called, in the future. Here are some further questions to ask myself:

What's calling me now?

_____
_____
_____
_____

What am I going to find or what am I hoping to find when I answer that call?

_____
_____
_____
_____

Warm Ups, Strength Training, and Cool Downs are equally important parts of a workout. The same is true for the exercises we have described in each of these sections. They are all very important to a successful regime and a well-balanced life. They help us deepen our relationship with ourselves.

After all, that is why we are here, isn't it? When we are ready to see our wholeness, the multiple dimensions that we occupy simultaneously and the beautiful way the Universe nurtures and prepares us, we can use the advanced workouts to further strengthen our spiritual muscles and become quite strong.

Section III

Solid Cornerstones

Accountability Builds Spiritual Character

Train yourself to think of and to look upon the world as something which is Becoming, which is growing; and to regard seeming evil as being only that which is undeveloped. Always speak in terms of advancement; to do otherwise is to deny your faith, and to deny your faith is to lose it.

~ Wallace D. Wattles

Who likes to be accountable? Who has a problem with unreliable people? Who would consider themselves reliable and dependable? What does accountability really mean?

We start out here as infants. Babies can't really be held accountable for who they are or what they do. We give them a very short window before we start holding them accountable for their actions. In other words: socialization.

We usually don't like that very much, at least not in the way we have seen or experienced parenting in the past. It is a rather difficult experience whether we are the parent or the child. As soon as we can get away from being parented, we generally go out on our own. Now we must be accountable to ourselves—or not. You can often tell who holds themselves accountable and who doesn't. Their lives are an indication of whether they let themselves off the hook with excuses why they can or cannot do something—*or* are dependable, rain or shine. These are the people who are stable and responsible in the way they live their lives. We quickly see who can be relied upon and who can't.

It's easy to look at others and make the call but it's a little more difficult to look at ourselves and evaluate our own actions. One of the key ingredients to our emotional and spiritual maturity is being able to do just that: look at ourselves not with harsh criticism and judgment, but from a detached objectivity where we can really be honest and teachable. We can't be so sensitive and protective as to take criticism personally. We need to take a closer look at our experiences so we can learn from them.

167

The question we need to ask is: How reliable or dependable am I... not only for others but for myself as well? We generally don't put our focus in that direction because we are so entertained and distracted by watching everyone else. We have to stop thinking so much about what is going on out therein the world and more about what is going on in here inside us, because our very own interior is the place where our reality begins and ends. Life really takes some interesting twists and turns depending on how reliable we are. If we aren't moving forward, it may be that we are stuck in a time warp, repeating history over and over again.

Ultimately, we do have to be accountable to our higher selves, to the Universe, to Spirit, to God. Even that really depends on how well we answer to ourselves.

Like most folks I learned accountability in stages over the course of my life. I was very shy in grade school. Sometime around fifth grade, significant growth occurred. I observed what other kids were doing and not doing to move ahead. I saw that I needed to get out of my shell and force myself to be more outgoing. I knew I needed to speak up for myself more. It was clear to me that if I didn't, life was going to pass me by.

How did I know that? I don't know. It wasn't like I was able to verbalize that at age 10. No one ever talked to me about it. It seemed to be an inner push by my higher self, wanting me to experience more of myself, and in doing so IT would experience more of ITself as well. The wisdom came in as my very own thoughts. Being left out or left behind was not a prospect I wanted to entertain. Even at that tender age, I started counting on myself to take on more responsibility for my own life.

I quickly understood that if I wanted something to happen in any area of my life, I was going to have to be the one to do it. I counted on myself for my first date. That wasn't happening without me, either. My dad was surely not helping. He was very strict with me as his firstborn daughter. From his own past experiences, he was well aware of the kinds of trouble kids can get into. He would have loved for me to never, ever date. (I now understand as a parent that he was just being protective of me. I guess his purpose was to help me avoid unnecessary trouble and have a greater chance of success. For that, I am most grateful.)

Attending an all-girls high school meant that we had to ask the guys out for our proms and dances. After much deliberation, I worked up the courage to ask Steve, a quiet football player from the nearby all-boys high school, to my junior prom. Thank God he said yes! If he hadn't, my dating would have been prolonged even more, which really wouldn't have been bad, except for the competition and pressure all around me. (They separated the girls from the boys so that we could focus on our studies, but the very opposite thing happened: most of us were boy *crazy* and thought of little else!)

I counted on myself to go to college. My parents didn't say a thing about it; they were too busy trying to keep up with a large family. (My mother went to college for a year when she was in the convent and enjoyed it very much. She would have liked to continue except she no longer wanted to be a nun. Even so, I don't remember her saying that I should go to college.)My high school graduation was coming up and I still didn't know what I was going to do.

Thank God that Colette, my best friend who lived down the street from us, had older siblings. She followed her older sister and brother and I tagged along right after her. I remember thinking that everyone was going somewhere but me. I had already worked retail and restaurants for years by this point and couldn't see myself doing that forever. Not wanting to be left behind and disappointed, I quickly got my act together, took the SAT and at the last minute applied to college and was accepted. I was so grateful that I did because I really loved it!

In more recent years, I had a dream which was really more of a nightmare. I found myself in another unhealthy relationship with someone I met during my divorce. I was ecstatic to wake up and realize this was only a dream! I was traumatized by it, nonetheless. Why was I having this dream? What was its message to me after all these years?

I had a heart-to-heart talk with myself: I have really put you through some things, haven't I? I am so sorry. I promise I will never do those things to you again. I will never compromise our health, well-being or security, nor put my family through those ordeals ever again. Everything we do affects those that are close to us, and I had pushed us all to the limits of what we could handle.

It felt so good to take ownership of that and know that I had grown enough to never allow that to happen again! It was an important realization for me. It was a part of my being able to count on myself.

We need confidence in ourselves that we will do the right thing. It is essential to know that we can count on ourselves. It all builds from there.

It's important to ask ourselves:

- How accountable have I been to myself?
- Have I been able to count on myself to be there when I really needed to be there for myself?
- What could I do to be more accountable for myself? After all, I was given "myself" to take care of through this lifetime.
- How am I doing with that?

The recent film, *Doctor Strange,* is quite metaphysical for a superhero movie. Doctor Strange is a surgeon who totally counted on himself and science to live his life. He thought he was invincible, and his life was centered on himself, though he did help others as a spinal cord/brain surgeon. One day he was involved in a car accident and lost the use of his hands. As a surgeon and musician his hands were everything to him. He felt there was no life left without them. The paradigms under which he was living had been shattered along with his hands. Science, as most of the world knows it, could take him no further.

He heard about a guru in India who might be able to help him heal his hands but was almost devastated to learn it wasn't possible. Instead he discovered a much larger world out there. He was trained to use his mind in new ways to access power sources from beyond what he ever knew previously. In his new life he became a powerful sorcerer, no longer attached to the idea that he needed his hands to live. Yes, it is a wild and crazy story! That's what I love about sci-fi. It plays with our imaginations. It is the classic hero's journey... textbook for us all, really.

There are as many different versions of this story as there are people. First we learn how to count on ourselves (even though we are never *just* depending on ourselves). Then there comes a time when we no longer can count on just ourselves. We must *consciously* count on a higher power. We must surrender to a higher power. It is only then that we can go on to create an even greater life for ourselves.

We can only really count on God, Life, the Universe, fully when we learn to count on ourselves, and that means putting ourselves out there. Instead of sitting around and waiting, we need to use what we have and see that there is more, even if it is different. The main gift has already been given. The setup is there. The raw materials are all around us, waiting to be used and put together in some interesting combinations. It's up to us to do something with it.

We become accountable to the Universe by appreciating the gift of life that we have, by loving, honoring and respecting ourselves...by living the best life we can possibly live.

The more we take responsibility for ourselves, for who we are, how we act and how we contribute to the world, the healthier, happier and more successful we will be. As we give our best in every possible way to life, we can count on Life being there totally for us. It already is...it just becomes an even greater presence for us to feel, see, touch and know.

When we fully count on ourselves in partnership with our Source, the Universe, new doors open for us that were not there before.

Spiritual practices build us up by deepening our relationship to our Source, helping us understand this partnership with Life, loving and caring for ourselves in a way that we might not have done before. Spiritual practices help us to be accountable to ourselves and to Life, which builds our spiritual character and stamina.

How accountable have I been to myself?

_____

_____

_____

_____

Have I been able to count on myself to be there when I really needed to be there for myself?

_____
_____
_____
_____

I was given myself to take care of through this life; what could I do to be more accountable for myself?

_____
_____
_____
_____

Examples of how I am accountable now:

1. _____
   _____
   _____
2. _____
   _____
   _____
3. _____
   _____
4. _____
   _____

Personal Journal Notes

_____

_____

_____

_____

A Well-trained Mind Supports Radiant Health &Well-being

If you wish health, watch your thoughts, not only about your physical being, but your thoughts about everything and everybody. With your will, keep them in line with your desire, and outwardly act in accordance with your thoughts, and you will soon realize that ALL power both over thoughts and conditions has been given to you.

~ Genevieve Behrend

If the forms of your thought are as vivid as the forms of nature, you are by virtue of the power of your imagination master of your fate.

~ Neville Goddard

Spiritual practices make a difference in our health and well-being. How responsible have we been for our health and well-being? For taking care of ourselves? For keeping our bodies and minds in shape to be able to live a greater life?

Surprisingly, workouts go way back to the ancient Greeks. Mind, body and spirit were key components to their lives. Dean Karnazes, author of *From Sparta to Today,* ran the Spartathlon, a 153-mile run from Athens to Sparta, which is one of the greatest physical feats in history. He discovered that the ancient Greeks exercised constantly, not just daily (that's *everyone*, not just athletes). They considered activity essential for life. Some spent their entire day at the gym (*gymnasium* is a Greek word). If they had to work, they made sure their business was near the gym so they could go as often as they could during their day. Today we would call such a person a fanatic or perhaps even obsessive compulsive. They didn't see it that way at all.

They had standing desks, which are becoming more popular again today to increase circulation in the body.

They practiced regular fasting and ate mostly plant-based foods.(Eating three square meals daily is a modern development.) Overeating, indulging and eating because it's time for a meal rather than because we are hungry are modern-day problems that did not exist for them.

Exercise was seen as play, restorative to the soul. They ran for the fun of it, trying different routes, sightseeing along the way...making a day of it.

They never stopped moving. Why? Because movement is life.

They knew how to enjoy life by living spontaneously, in the moment.

That lifestyle alone would create more healthy and balanced people, physically and mentally. Their basic health was supported, preparing them to experience a greater life.

Are there some changes we could make that would help us shift into a healthier lifestyle? Could we be more active? Taking responsibility for ourselves physically puts us in a better frame of mind and gives us a lifestyle that is sustainable and feels supportive.

It's interesting that viruses can't reproduce on their own; they need a host to multiply. What's to keep us all from being hosts to undesirable viruses? Strong, healthy, happy, resilient, balanced and harmonious bodies are what protect us. Where can we get a body like that?! We all want one. Who couldn't do without sickness and disease? There's lots of talk these days about health and what we need to do to stay healthy. Health is a major part of our lives. Not feeling well can really put a damper on the quality of our life.

Most of us are born strong and resilient, which carries us for quite some time. As we go, the body begins to break down— *not* because the body itself ages, but because we don't have the kind of thinking that is supportive of our health. Because of our inexperience, we take for granted the body we have been given, thinking it will always be there, that we can do whatever we want with it and nothing will ever happen. Until it does!

When something does happen, we are surprised. Our fallback explanation changes to:"This is a part of life, "or" It was my turn to get something."Not necessarily so!

The longer we are around, the more opportunities we have for things to go wrong. Why? Because our bodies are an outward manifestation of what is going on inside of us. As our life continues, there's even more going on in our inner world, isn't there? In fact, many times there's a buildup of things going on that have not been properly processed or dealt with. Hence, our unfinished business comes out in disturbing ways as physical ailments or conditions.

Most often, we don't know how to manage our feelings and emotions. Our fears, worries and concerns cause the real wear and tear on us. How we talk *to* ourselves and how we talk *about* ourselves play a part in our health and well-being. We can keep that under wraps for quite some time, even from ourselves, but eventually it begins to show up in our bodies. The body doesn't lie. It can't. It gives us a picture of what is going on and what we need help with. Our energy plays a significant part in how we look and feel.

- How can we keep the health we have or enhance it?
- How can we restore our health to be all it could be?
- How can we have an even greater idea of health than we currently think is possible?

Health is a very personal matter. It's really no one else's business. No one has a right to judge what is going on with another. It is *our* concern because we are responsible for our own bodies. It's *our* business where we are with them and what we need to do about them. We need to be very kind and gentle with ourselves and each other when it comes to the subject of our health. Learning more about how these bodies work and what they need is important. Learning about the mind-body connection is another level of learning that is worth our while because it increases our chances of maximizing our physical well-being.

To support those ideas, it is essential that we get the facts straight about our health from a spiritual point of view, which will give us an even greater advantage when it comes to building strong bodies. The spiritual truth is:

- The truth is that God...Good...Life... is all there is, everywhere equally present, all knowing and all powerful. That means in our minds and bodies as well.

- The truth is that health is our natural state of being. It is our birthright. Health is our truth.
- The truth is that *we* are first cause to our own experience. There is no truth to our being a victim of anything or powerless in any way. The personal factor made up of our thoughts and beliefs determines what health challenges we may or may not face.
- The truth is that health is a decision and a way of life... a life filled with a healthy mind and loving thoughts (as much as possible).

Spirit is vibrant health and wholeness, and therefore I am vibrant health and wholeness, because I am of Spirit. Spirit's truth is my truth. I am already whole! Practicing those thoughts so that we can experience them puts us into alignment with our inner being, which is our natural state of being. Alignment with our higher self re-establishes our body to its perfection.

What a difference it would make if we could get our minds straight about this! We are in the beginning stages of really understanding how spiritual truth affects everything. It's time to reflect on what we know and are doing.

How am I keeping the health I have or enhancing it?

_____

_____

_____

_____

How am I restoring my health to be all it could be?

_____

_____

_____

_____

How can I have an even greater idea of health than I currently think is possible?

_____

_____

As we achieve a greater understanding of the mind-body connection, we will claim personal power regarding our health and well-being. Then the answers and solutions will become clear. Knowing this and how Life works will more than strengthen our spiritual muscles... we will shine because we are experiencing radiant health.

Personal Journal Notes

_____

_____

_____

_____

_____

_____

_____

_____

_____

_____

_____

_____

Spiritual Strength Leads to Prosperous Living

One who understands others has knowledge;
one who understands himself has wisdom.

Mastering others requires force;
mastering the self needs strength.

If you realize that you have enough, you are truly rich.

One who gives himself to his position surely lives long.
One who gives himself to the Tao surely lives forever.
~ 33rd verse of the Tao Te Ching

Spiritual practices are tools that help us understand ebb and flow. They give us the spiritual wisdom to generously use what we have and to attract even more. Life is one big circulatory system, entirely interconnected. This section introduces some tools to help us deal with money. See Chapter 7 in *I Can Do This Thing Called Life and So Can You!* for more information on Wealth.

Someone told me recently how he got into some trouble with credit cards when he was young. Well into adulthood, he thought he couldn't be trusted with keeping track of his bills and money. When he got married it was easier to let his partner, who was stronger in that area, take over and not have anything to do with it ever again... or so he thought. That system worked until they divorced. Then the responsibility fell on him again.

At first, he was afraid to look at his bank balance. He didn't want to know where things stood because he didn't believe it could be good. Little by little, through his spiritual practices and encouragement from a new friend, he grew in confidence about handling his money. He started taking more responsibility for this once difficult area of his life, and today he feels great about where he is financially. He knows he is on the right track. In fact, he is doing so well that his financial picture now surpasses his wildest dreams.

We, too, can grow in our confidence about the area of finances and how we handle our resources. It may be the last thing we want to do. We may not have a clue where to start. Yet, if we have a willingness to stick with it and keep a positive attitude, we will see positive results.

A truth is that our problem is never really about money, anyway. Money is not the solution to our difficulties, even though we think it would make a difference having some. Having great sums of money can take us comfortably from point A to point B, but having it may prevent the very thing that needs to happen: that shift in our consciousness, a greater belief in ourselves, knowing that we can do what we really want to do. We can enjoy it all. We were meant to be happy. Money can't do that for us. Only we can do that for ourselves. It never really was about money.

What do you mean it isn't about money? The problem is that we have that belief.

The problem really isn't about money. The problem is the way we think. The way we're thinking about ourselves, about money and about the flow of life are what get in the way of our having more. Changes in our thought process help us relinquish our old patterns of thought, making something new possible.

We were never meant to live in limitation. We were never meant to have to watch every penny that we spend. We were never meant to have to bargain hunt as a way of life, or be afraid of someone taking advantage of us, or pay our bills late, or hold onto our money because we don't know when we will have some again.

The Power of Giving

Becoming comfortable with the flow of money coming in and going out does take some getting used to. Of course we like to see the money coming in. Sometimes, though, we don't feel as comfortable with money going out, especially if we don't know how or whether more will come in. The ache, the void, the loss we feel when the tide goes out is often mistaken as bad. We say, "Oh look. Here I am again. My checkbook is empty. I am back where I started. I always end up here. Why does this always happen to me?"

But this is merely our misinterpretation of what is going on. We live in an intelligent Universe. We must approach every subject intelligently. By that I mean we must know how Life works and how we can work together with It.

With energy, love, work, and our good, if we could see that ebb is part of a cycle, just as much as flow, we would realize that it is normal. If we saw that it is very much like breathing air out of our lungs, we wouldn't become so worried. We could continue to breathe and not skip a beat. We wouldn't get stuck or panic because we would know that a breath out means another breath in. We can't keep taking air in without letting air out. We can't keep taking in our good, our money, our energy, our love, without expressing and circulating it. We would explode or burst.

Take a breath in and then release it. This is how the Universe works. Just like breathing, we don't need to jump to conclusions, think the worst, and spiral down from there. We just need to keep focused on the idea that this is how life was designed.

Living without giving is not part of the Divine Health Care Plan or the Universal Bank, whichever way we want to look at it. If we could see how normal this cycle is, we would relax and go with it instead of freaking out. It would become second nature to us, just like breathing.

With each gift we give or intend to give, we receive immediately. The getting is in the giving, and we receive immediately by our own act. We feel good about ourselves. We are open to a greater circulation of good. We create a vacuum that will be quickly replaced with something equivalent or of greater value than what we have given. Giving always comes before getting. We must sow the seed before we can reap the harvest. What we plant today we will soon harvest. Guaranteed. That's the way life works.

Instead of living life from a place of "What's in it for me?" our question needs to be "What kind of contribution can I make to my world and to all those around me?"The answer to that positions us for greater good. It's not that we shouldn't get what we want – we should. Going about it from a higher consciousness puts us into alignment with the Universe. Anything that puts us into greater alignment is worthy of our attention because it helps us increase the outcome of our desire. Our emphasis needs to be on what we bring to the table of life. Then we can discover what our purpose is and what will naturally come into our lives when we come to life each day as a giver.

> *You must stop spending your thoughts, your time and your money. Everything in life must be an investment.*
> ~ Neville Goddard

What kind of contribution can I make to my world and to all those around me?

_____
_____
_____
_____

The Power of Creativity

We were born to create. Some people might say, "Well, how can I create when I don't have any money?" or "I would love to do this or that, but I don't have any money." What do we do when we find ourselves in a situation where we're born to create (because it's our nature to create), we want to do things, and we need the resources to do them?

We begin by spending time thinking about the experience we desire. We could envision what we would like to see happen for us. We can ask ourselves, "What does experiencing this feel like? What could it do for me? What could it do for my family and those around me?"

Continuing to use money as an example, many of us still fall under the belief that we must attract the money before we can do the things we want to do, leaving us impotent to begin our plans. We even spend our lives waiting for ways to make them happen.

In the spiritual sense, it works the other way around. If we get clear and focus on the good ideas we want to experience, we will naturally and easily attract either the divine substance we call money or some other way to implement our plans. The thing that few people know is that *money follows a good idea.* It's not the other way around. It's NOT: "I will do this *when* I have the money, or when my ship comes in."

Money – divine substance – comes with the package of what is being created, in the same way the components necessary to grow a tall oak tree are found within the acorn in combination with the sun, soil and water. The seed contains the nucleus which defines the plan. The same is true for the desires we want to manifest. The means to the support for our desire are already there within the idea. The means to carry out our desire are there to the degree that we believe they are. Divine Substance abounds and appears in the forms we need such as money, energy, love or whatever else we seek. The more time we spend developing our idea in mind, the more resources will be attracted to us. Our job is to get into the consciousness of what we are creating. The rest will take care of itself.

Spending time writing down our ideas or imaging them in our minds is a beneficial use of our energy. Looking at pictures to get ideas about the thing we want and imagining ourselves as the recipient of whatever beauty and goodness it is, provides a nucleus which attracts to us everything needed.

This is the way an intelligent Universe works: things come from all different places and channels to help us manifest our desires without question. Why? Because Life ITself wants to experience them, as us. God, Spirit, Life, is responsible for our desiring nature.

This co-creation we engage in together, as one, is the creation process. Life brings together everything needed to help support our ideas. We don't necessarily have to make the money before our plans can come to fruition. We do need to spend time thinking behind the scenes about the picture we want to experience, becoming very clear about what we want to see, what it feels like to have it and then claiming it as ours in the present moment before we ever see it. That will bring it to life for us more quickly than ever.

The Power of Self Care

There are so many things that we have accepted and tolerated because we have grown up with those limiting ideas about the world and how it operates. We don't question them. We don't think we can do anything about our current financial status because that's the way it is. We do all kinds of things for money at the expense of our health and well-being. We put up with things for the wrong reasons that we should never tolerate when we can have all the financial wealth we could ever need or want and enjoy doing what we love. Isn't that great to know?

So, if we want to see prosperous results in our lives, we can spend time doing what uplifts us. A good question to ask every day is: *"What do I need to know or do today that will give me a greater sense of freedom, make me feel good and help me feel proud?"* Then we can listen and do what we feel guided to do.

The answer can be anything. If lighting a candle helps us feel like we are capturing a sacred moment, then we should light a candle. It could be enjoying fresh-cut flowers from our garden or treating ourselves to a nice meal... anything that makes us feel special. Taking good care of ourselves is essential. Just going through the motions of paying the bills will not get us as far as bringing our heart and soul into the act. When we do that, we turn the experience into a sacred experience of gratitude and appreciation.

Even if it's just a few minutes a day, taking time for ourselves gives us the message that there is time for us. It's part of loving ourselves. Everything else can be put on hold while we choose to do something that frees us up spiritually. Whatever we choose to do is good for us. When our own cup is filled to overflowing, we are open to life's possibilities.

The more we do what we want to do, the more we will see and feel our greater alignment with Life's flow. We'll get ideas to go here, or go there, as we put ourselves in greater circulation. The clearer we become about who we are, what our purpose is, and the value we bring to the world, the more we will be a magnet for possibility, opportunity and success in every area of our lives. Life will not be able to resist us because we have become irresistible!

Am I ready to live a more prosperous life? _____

What action steps could I take that would be making a greater investment in myself and my life?

_____

_____

_____

_____

The Power Working With Us

Our ache, our pain, our yearning is the sacred in us wanting to be closer to the Divine. When we feel that way, it is an opportunity for us to go deeper. When we have a greater understanding of what is going on, we can address it in a more spiritually mature way. That will help us stay in touch with our inner resources that will enable us to stay in the flow.

When we find ourselves in doubt or fear, we can ask, "What is that about?" Doubt is our inability to believe we can have whatever we want. Fear is really the lack of love. Lack of love puts us out of alignment with our true, infinite self. There is a great I AM within us, a knower that knows all. That great presence of Spirit, of Light, of God within us guides our way.

Whenever we feel that it's just us, our "small I" self, our personality that must make it all happen, we are thinking that it's all up to us. We believe we not only have to dream the dream, but also raise the money and control the outcome every step of the way. It's all up to us and nothing is going to happen unless *we* do it. Working from that mindset can be tiresome and frustrating. We were never meant to do it all. There is a part for us to do and there is a part for Source to do. We must learn to get our parts right and let IT do what IT does best. Otherwise we will continue to feel separate and alone and have a hard time ever believing that good can be ours.

The truth is that we are not in this life alone. We are interconnected. We cannot be separated or abandoned. We must know that we are working with an Infinite Partner that knows everything there is to know about orchestrating and organizing a plan that will bring together whatever we want to experience.

The more that we can remember to use that Infinite Partner, the more we will see things demonstrate right before our eyes from the tiniest detail to the grandest, full-blown, amazing picture.

One woman I know went food shopping once a week. Her son counted on having a pickle for his lunch every day, and her daughter just happened to eat the very last one. I know that doesn't sound like much to fuss about, but between siblings it can be an issue. The mother stood her ground, saying quietly that she was not going back to the store, and turned the issue over to the Higher Power. She let the Universe take care of her son's needs. Sure enough, a lone pickle found its way into their house at just the time it was needed. The Universe came up with a way for that to happen. How? A family member brought home a sandwich they bought and they didn't want the pickle that came with it. Voila! A pickle appeared where there was none before. Everything worked out to perfection!

Nothing is too big or too small to expect if we believe and let the Universe do ITs thing. Yes, even a pickle is not too much to ask! Better to practice on the small things to build up our spiritual muscles in preparation for the larger things. It's not that the larger things are more difficult to manifest, but they are usually harder for us to believe possible.

The Power of Awareness

Those of us from the U.S. are some of the richest people on the planet. Some estimate that even our poor are in the top ten percent of the world's richest people. While this is difficult to believe, looking at things this way helps us keep the right perspective no matter what is going on in our lives.

But that doesn't mean we can't expect or accept more. The quality of our lives and our feeling of aliveness is our gauge for how much prosperity we can enjoy. Knowing we live in a world of infinite possibilities can keep us going when things seem rough or when we need a better idea.

The reality is that there is always something greater trying to happen. Something else is possible that we could be experiencing. That mindset keeps us going. That's what keeps us living big! That kind of thinking keeps us alive and vital.

When we make the most of what we have, whether it be love, energy, our presence, or our wealth, we put ourselves in a greater flow with Life. The very act of giving immediately gives us a greater sense of prosperity. Feeling a greater sense of abundance is a draw for substance to flow to us. There is always something for us to give, whether it be a phone call or a thank-you note. It's the little things that can make all the difference.

May we all live a life of greater ease, joy and prosperity!

Personal Journal Notes

_____

_____

_____

_____

_____

_____

_____

_____

_____

_____

_____

_____

_____

Spiritual Development Moves Us to Greater Expression

My mind is a center of Divine operation. The Divine operation is always for expansion and fuller expression, and this means the production of something beyond what has gone before, something entirely new, not included in the past experience, though proceeding out of it by an orderly sequence of growth.

Therefore, since the Divine cannot change its inherent nature, it must operate in the same manner with me; consequently, in my own special world, of which I am the center, it will move forward to produce new conditions, always in advance of any that have gone before.

~ Thomas Troward

Work and Life

What is work, and how can we get to a place where it's not something we dread but instead becomes something we cherish? How can we take the beautiful words of Khalil Gibran in his book *The Prophet*, "Work is love made visible," and make them real for us? Work can be so much more than what we have been brought up thinking. Maybe we need a better idea about what we call our work.

The dictionary defines *work* this way:

Work is activity involving mental or physical effort, done in order for us to achieve a purpose or result.

In other words, work is an activity requiring mental or physical effort in order to achieve a desired effect. It doesn't describe what kind of mental or physical effort. Because we have been programmed to think this means it must be a strain,

189

struggle or hardship, that often is what we experience. When we can look upon work in a much more satisfying way, we will reap more gratifying results.

We may think we need a job because we need to earn a living. While it is true that we have a responsibility to contribute to the greater good of all by participating in some way, it is not true that we must work to earn a living or have an income. Work *may* be a way that we accomplish both. Work does get us out into circulation in the world and connects us with others. It does help us earn a living by doing our part. But if we go back to the definition: *Work is an activity involving mental or physical effort, done in order for us to achieve a purpose or result,* we see that pretty much describes *everything* we do during our waking hours.

Life is all about mental and physical effort! Our days are filled with it. Everything we do is mental and physical to varying degrees. Every little thing we do, all day long, is for a purpose, whether it be doing laundry or preparing food. It seems we must expand our view of the word *work* to one of *life.*

I remember being stuck in a miserable place to work when I first moved to Atlanta after my divorce. The work involved accounting, which I rather liked, but the environment was horrible. My self-image was so shaken by all I had been through! I felt I had to take the position. I found myself stuck in an environment where I literally could not breathe. (This was the early '80s when people were still allowed to smoke in the workplace.) Yet I couldn't just quit without having another job; I needed the money. And, even though I sent out dozens of resumes, nothing seemed to give. I saw no other way than to stay put.

At my lowest point, I heard these priceless words by my teacher, Dr. Kennedy Shultz: "If you want to get out of something, you have to get into it." That got my attention. I had never heard that before. They were not the words I wanted to hear, but when I heard them, I knew they were true: my ticket out. He was the expert, and I decided it best to follow his advice. I stopped complaining, whining and dreading... which wasn't getting me anywhere. I decided to experiment with bringing my best love and attention to myself and everyone else, including my work. I did everything in my power to adhere to my new resolve, and that did the trick. I was out of there in six weeks! Even though the company finally bought some small ventilation machines, it didn't really help. It was my time to go. You can imagine how ecstatic I was to leave there!

If we are to get out of any undesirable relationship, environment, situation or thing, we must first get into it. If we are ever to see new and better results, *we* must come from a better place with it all.

What do I need to "get into" in order to "get out of" the work I am in and attract something greater?

_____

_____

_____

_____

What qualities express the kind of work I would love?

1. _____
2. _____
3. _____
4. _____
5. _____

The Happiness Project

Gretchen Rubin, author of *The Happiness Project,* wanted more out of her life than she was experiencing. She had the idea to start a year-long happiness project as a way of inviting change. Each month she focused on some different aspect: energy boosting, love, aiming higher, lightening up, etc. This was an experiment to see if focusing in a specific way would make a difference. At the end of the year she would examine whether she was, indeed, happier.

In her month on aiming higher she discovered, "Happiness is a critical factor for work, and work is a critical factor for happiness." Happy people out-perform unhappy people. They work harder and longer and are friendlier, easier to work with, more willing to help others and more likely to be leaders.

Work, if looked at from a higher perspective, satisfies our sense of belonging, of having a purpose, of being recognized. These are key things we can't get any other way. When happiness and work come together, people take notice. Love is made visible to all around.

Gretchen also searched for a role model, and she found St. Thérèse of Lisieux, a French woman who was born in 1873. St. Thérèse had received special permission from Pope John Paul I to enter the convent at the age of 15. She spent nine years cloistered with 20 other nuns until she died of tuberculosis. In the story of her life, *Story of a Soul,* she wrote:

Love proves itself by deeds, so how am I to show my love? Great deeds are forbidden me (being cloistered from the world). The only way I can prove my love is by... every little sacrifice, every glance, and word, and the doing of the least actions for love.

Thérèse went on to show that an ordinary life, even a cloistered one, was full of opportunities to prove love. There was one sister that everyone disliked. Everything she did got under everyone's skin. She decided to prove her love to God by running to this nun at every turn and not avoiding her as everyone else did. Thérèse decided to treat this sister as though she were her favorite. What a difference that made!

In her journals she wrote, "For the love of God and my sisters (so charitable toward me), I take care to appear happy, and especially to be so." She became so good at seeming happy and laughing that many of the nuns had trouble seeing virtue in what appeared to come so natural to her. They had no idea that she, too, had to work at it. What an example of loving no matter what, and emphasizing our own responsibility to be happy for ourselves and for those around us she was! She went on to be made a doctor and one of the 33 super saints of the Catholic Church.

What is love if it is not shared?
~ Jennifer Worth, in the television series *Call the Midwife*

By the end of the project year, Gretchen had taken a long, hard look at her life, what made her feel good, what made her feel bad, what was right and what felt like growth, and she decided that she was indeed happier. Her life and the life of her family had changed considerably from this project. She worked it from every angle and got the rewards she was looking for. Love was made visible. She invites us to create our own happiness project and see where it takes us.

One Hundred Percent

A younger friend of mine had been riding the fence for a long time, as we all have done. Her new mantra is, "One Hundred Percent." She's watching what's coming out of her mouth and what she is allowing in from the outside. She says even the songs we grew up with have words that no longer match who we are today. She's going cold turkey on the negative and cleaning up her life. One Hundred Percent – no excuses. That's a spiritual practice. That's dedication!

Our greatest work is what we do with ourselves. We are known by "our works."If there's good stuff being generated within us, everyone can see it. There is no hiding what is going on within us for very long. We will be giving our gift to the world. We won't be able to stop ourselves from giving, it will feel so good.

We enter into the Spirit of Life only as we enter into the Spirit of Giving!

~ Ernest Holmes

When the quality of our efforts improves, things change. Even more, we change. When we make a greater investment in Life, Life takes us more seriously and makes a greater investment in us!

Ancient wisdom tells us that faith without works is dead. How we express ourselves to the world around us is a good part of who we are. Finding a new way to look at everything we do positions us to attract more engaging and enlightening opportunities that can only feed our soul.

Personal Journal Notes

Recharging Our Spiritual Energy Opens Us to Greater Love

In the depth of winter, I finally learned that within me there lay an invincible summer.

~ Albert Camus

A merry heart doeth good like a medicine, but a broken spirit drieth the bones.

Proverbs 17:22

Awe is what moves us forward.

~ Joseph Campbell

I was particularly touched upon hearing the vows of my nephew and his wife at their wedding. They called each other best friends. It was clear to see they had something very special. Whether in a marriage, partnership or friendship, love is exemplified by bringing people together. Nothing gets in the way of Love. It fills us. It takes over.

It's easy to see love and feel it when we look at a couple who are making a commitment to each other. It's harder to see a loved one struggling. My nephew's own brother had just returned from Iraq, still struggling for his life with an addiction to heroin. It was so good to see him standing next to his big brother; all dressed up, handsome as ever. He reminded me of a younger version of my dad. I got to enjoy watching him as he escorted people to their seats, smiling. Maybe, just maybe, he caught a glimpse of a bigger life for himself, connecting with his cousins and family... feeling the love we all have for each other.

Watching all of this happening, I whispered to my son Nick, who was sitting by my side, "Let's remember him like this. Let's remember him happy."

Whoever has Love has Life and radiates Life wherever they walk.

Whoever gets into a state of overflowing, unquenchable love is manifesting the Christ Self. In that state we see no evil in anybody or anything, seeing only their Good.

~ Emma Curtis Hopkins

In Emerson's essay, "Circles," he refers to St. Augustine's description of God as being a circle whose center is everywhere and whose circumference is nowhere. There can be no circle drawn around God and God's center is everywhere. Therefore, *Love must already be right where we are.* It's up to us to recognize it.

Love is never something we have to go out and get. Love is always something we have, and the more we give it away, use it and express it, the more it returns. Spiritual law guarantees that what we give out will circle back.

At this wedding, I also got to spend time with my ex-husband and his wife… very nice people. Our divorce was more than 25 years before. The Universe gave me a glimpse of what my life might have looked like had we stayed together. It was clear that I was living the life I was meant to be living. It didn't necessarily look like it from an outsider's perspective, but I knew in my heart it was true. I was living the life for me. They are happy. I am happy. It's all perfect. I got to see how far I had come.

Love always returns to where it started better for where it has been!

~ Kennedy Shultz

A few weeks before this wedding, our daughter, Liz, had a dream that she saw her deceased grandmother (my mom) at the wedding. Of course, I knew Mom would be there. I am sure Dad was there too, appreciating from the other side how well and large and beautiful their family was. There was a slideshow of each side of the family and sure enough, Mom was there in two of the pictures, looking as beautiful as ever.

The more I thought about it, I realized that it was the special love my parents shared with each other that was responsible for us all being here on this momentous occasion. Fifty-seven years before, Mom wrote a letter to Dad (he was in the army before they married): "Bill, all I ask is to be a help to you first, spiritually and second, to make life on earth as pleasant for you as possible."

That she did. They were very close. There was another part in her letter about striving to put God first and each other second. Their love, dedication, and hard work led to 5 children, 16 grandchildren and so far, 7 great-grandchildren.

Whatever their beliefs or interpretations of God and what they were meant to do, their intention to love and come from the highest possible place created a powerful result. They live. Their love lives. It will go on forever. When I looked around the room at the happy faces, my heart was filled with joy. There was a newness to our family and our future that was encouraging and inspirational.

The Stream of Life

The same stream of life that runs through my veins, runs through the world and dances in rhythmic measure.

It is the same life that shoots in joy through the dust of the earth into numberless blades of grass and breaks into tumultuous waves of leaves and flowers.

It is the same life that is rocked in the ocean cradle of birth and death, in ebb and flow.

My limbs are made glorious by the touch of this world of life. My pride is from the life throb of ages, dancing in my blood this moment.

~ Rabindranath Tagore

Love is all there is. This never-ending love of which we are all a part continues to feed, grow, nourish and expand us. It will keep on going forever. Our own legacies, however humble, have longevity to them. The love we give keeps on going forever. There's no better spiritual practice than to exercise our muscles by loving more. As we do, the energy of Love Itself takes over in us and gives us an invincible strength.

Am I open and receptive to greater love in my life?
_____

How can I be more loving to myself and those around me?
_____
_____
_____
_____

Personal Journal Notes

_____

_____

_____

_____

_____

_____

_____

_____

_____

_____

_____

_____

Spiritual Maturity Deepens Our Relationship with the Infinite

Only that Illumined One
Who keeps seducing the formless into form
Had the charm to win my Heart.
Only a Perfect One
Who is always Laughing at the word TWO
Can make you know of Love.

~ Hafiz

Unable to perceive the shape of you,
I find you all around me.
Your presence fills my eyes with your love,
It humbles my heart, for you are everywhere.

~ Hakim Sanai

Connecting with Home

A couple of years ago, I went to Wisconsin to welcome my new twin granddaughters, Aubrey and Everly, into the world... pure spirits fresh from the other side. I had no idea what to expect or how I really felt about becoming a grandmother. Two baby girls showed up for our very first round, which made me even more apprehensive. I guessed I would find out when I got there.

I also had a chance to see and spend time with my brother and sister-in-law, Mike and Betty. A visit was in order. Until now, raising our third child and co-directing a center, getting away had been difficult for me. I scheduled two visits to maximize my trip. Relationships can withstand a lot of neglect, but truly I was in the hole regarding my brother. It didn't help that I had responded negatively to a political email he sent me. That was a sure way to shut down communication. What can I say? I had a moment! I am divine, and human, too.

Meeting the babies and staying with my daughter and her guy was very special. It was also constant feeding, diaper changing and cooking. All three of us were in motion continuously. After the first week together, I decided that a weekend away would give the new family a chance to bond and grant me an opportunity to see my brother, sister-in-law, and even some friends of 50 years.

I arrived in Milwaukee at the beautiful downtown bus station. I was content to sit and read my book while waiting for my brother to finish work and pick me up. My phone rang. It was my oldest son, Nick, calling in response to a text I had sent him earlier as I passed by Waukesha, where he had attended college.

"Mom," he said, "You can't sit in a bus station. Find the Third Ward. Find the Hinterland [a high-end restaurant he started up years ago and managed at one time]. They are so close. I am not even going to talk to you until you find them. Call me back when you do."

I knew he was right. It was good for me to get out on the streets and take advantage of the opportunity before me, so I followed Nick's orders. I got out my trusty phone and discovered that the Third Ward, a very popular district of downtown, was indeed only minutes away, as he said. I walked through the marketplace, seeing and smelling all kinds of delicious foods. It was an "OMG" moment! I savored the feast around me without even having a bite... too many choices... fresh cheeses, meats, seafood, smoothies, baked goods and more! How fabulous! As much as I didn't miss long winters in the north, I did miss the different ethnic foods on which I was raised. I called Nick and thanked him profusely for making me get out into the city! Whatever was I thinking, to sit safely in the bus station, even if it was beautiful and new?

Shortly afterward, Mike pulled up in his car. There is something so wonderful about seeing someone you grew up with and haven't seen in awhile! Born only 11 months after I was, he is the person I have known the longest, except for a few older relatives. Every year we are the same age for the month of July. He looked good. He and his wife had just learned that they were going to be grandparents, too – with twins, no less! How crazy is that? Twins haven't appeared in our family for a couple of generations, and then two sets of them within six months of each other? Unbelievable!

He proceeded to take me on a tour of the city... going past all of the places we lived, all of the schools I attended, our church (Whitnall Park, one of our favorite hangouts, and the first church of my choice). Memories rushed in of our early days and of a life long gone. Because I had done so much healing within myself, I could take it all in and enjoy it. My past flashed before my eyes like a life review. I had to ask myself, *Am I going somewhere?* The best part of all this was that I was still alive to really get into this with the one person who knew all my history and could relate. Later that evening we had a fun dinner with his wife, Betty.

The next night was set aside for my friend Colette and her husband, Skip, whom I have known forever. She asked me where I wanted to go and I replied, "I don't have a clue. I don't even know what is here anymore." She gave me the choice of going down to the waterfront and art center or going to Holy Hill and Fox & Hounds Restaurant outside the city.

A chill ran through me when she mentioned the latter. My Great-uncle Willie used to visit from St. Louis, where my mother and her family were from. He always stayed at a hotel with an indoor pool so all of us kids could go swimming, year-round. We loved when Uncle Willie came to town! It became a family tradition that he would take us for Mass to Holy Hill, a very special cathedral, and for lunch afterward at the famous Fox & Hounds Restaurant.

Without hesitation, I responded to my friend, "Fox and Hounds." She proceeded to say, "We can leave early, see the sunset, and stop at Holy Hill before dinner." I was beside myself! We didn't quite make it before sunset but driving toward the sunset as the sky darkened was a spectacular sight. Seeing the cathedral all lit up on top of the hill was like seeing a castle. I had never seen it at nightfall. It was breathtaking!

We had the most wonderful evening! A beautiful dinner with friends I could really be myself with. What they shared about themselves and what they had been through touched my heart. We brought up memories that had long been forgotten. Being with them really fed my soul and renewed our connection.

It helped me see that these were precious relationships that would endure forever.

The next day my sister messaged my siblings that she had found a holy card (while rummaging through a drawer looking for something else) belonging to my mother that included the date of her transition. It was *that* exact day, nine years ago. The orchestration of the whole weekend was so perfect. It seemed as though my mother played a part in bringing us all together.

I was also treated to waking one morning to a beautiful first snow of the season. Silent, fragile, indescribable snowflakes fell, covering all. I still love watching a snowfall!

After that wonderful weekend, I returned to my daughter and her family. It's interesting that babies' eyes can only see images and shadows. Learning to see is a process like learning how to walk. Experts say it may take babies one to two years to see like we see and learn to interpret what they see. Even getting both eyes to work together in unison is quite a feat. In my opinion, that alone would explain why newborns cry so much. There is so much to acclimate to when we come into this world. How frustrating it must be!

I did what I could in the way of reassuring and comforting. First, sitting in the rocker with Everly, I told her,

- How magnificent she was...
- How everything will be okay...
- How she and her twin came in together to love and support one another...
- How they must have come here to do great things to bring in such reinforcements...together, and not alone...
- How I would always be there for her, no matter what, even when I am gone from here...

Then, standing with Aubrey, looking out the patio door at the open field, I told her,

- How magnificent she was...
- How everything will be okay...
- How she and her twin came in together to love and support one another...

- How they must have come here to do great things to bring in such reinforcements...together, and not alone...
- How I would always be there for her, no matter what, even when I am gone from here...

I spoke to them both of things they couldn't possibly see or understand yet, and even still, I knew I was talking to their spirits, which are infinite and forever.

It hit me, while comforting Aubrey, that *I* was surrounded by and being comforted and assured by a presence or being that knows and loves me, that clearly sees who I am and knows of the great things yet to be for me and that everything will be okay. It will all be good.

Just as *I* was there for the babies and others, something more was there, appreciating *me* in that same moment. I couldn't help but smile and decided I could take that idea in and be comforted by it. I would remember that Source is always there for me, too! I could be open to more love and acceptance.

Like the babies, we also have frustrating moments. Sometimes it takes us years to see clearly what for so long had been unclear and confusing. What if we could talk to ourselves as I spoke to these babies?

Imagine with me for a moment, someone telling *you*...

- How magnificent you are...

- How everything will be okay...

- How you must have come here to do great things...

- How they will always be there for you, no matter what...

They know of things you couldn't possibly see or understand yet, and even still, they speak to the Great Spirit of you, which is infinite and forever.

We can also do that exercise with ourselves and our higher self or God.

Spiritual Beings

When you become deeply interested in spiritual evolution, the universe becomes even more interested in you. And when you put the intention to evolve above and beyond all else, it's the greatest gift you can give to God--a partner in the evolutionary process emerges in the form of YOU.

~ Alan Cohen

Why are so many of us frustrated with what we see and hear going on around us? It's because we have gone as far as we *can* go without a better understanding of love.

Without a better understanding of who we are as spiritual beings, and without knowing and utilizing the real love and support that is here for us, we can only do so much.

As I wrote in my book, *I Can Do This Thing Called Life and So Can You!,*

The One that is Love and that created us has all the answers. The solutions are available to us. They are waiting for you and me to get ready for them, and when we do, we will not be disappointed.

I could not have planned or coordinated all the precious moments and interactions that took place during my trip to Wisconsin. They just happened. It is rare for things to play out with that kind of precision and detail, capturing a life review that would have taken years to plan if it were merely up to me. Spirit was clearly in charge. During my spiritual practice beforehand, my intention was to:

- Make this trip count.
- Know that money was no object.
- Have a meaningful connection with my brother, his wife and my friends and of course, be with my daughter and her new family.
- Come from love no matter what.

I also had worked on any past issues that came up beforehand, so I was free to savor it all. I got so much more out of my time away than I put into it or even thought possible.

Something I've experienced that couldn't be explained and would fall under the category of spiritual is:

_____

_____

_____

_____

An Inner Realization

What the world needs is spiritual conviction followed by spiritual experience. I would rather see a student of this Science prove its Principle than to have him repeat all the words of wisdom that have ever been uttered. It is far easier to teach the Truth than it is to practice it.

But the practice of Truth is personal to each, and in the long run no one can live our life for us. To each is given what he needs and the gifts of heaven come alike to all. How we shall use these gifts is all that matters! To hold one's thought steadfastly to the constructive, to that which endures, and to the Truth, may not be easy in a rapidly changing world, but to the one who makes the attempt much is guaranteed.

The essence of spiritual mind healing--and of all true religious philosophy--is an inner realization of the Presence of Perfection within and around about. It is the hope of heaven, the Voice of God proclaiming, "I AM that which thou art; thou art that which I AM."

~ Ernest Holmes

These are gifts of a different kind, such as I experienced during my visit with family and friends, that we can give ourselves – true gifts of Life. As we do, the world as we know it will transform because we are living life on our terms. Everyone else benefits in seeing us succeed.

Make the most of this time! Enjoy the gift that you are! Put yourself first and then give from your overflow. Spiritual practices and making lifestyle changes that support us make it easy for us to have an up close and personal relationship with the Infinite.

Do I have a relationship with my inner self?

_____

Personal Journal Notes

_____

_____

_____

_____

_____

_____

_____

_____

_____

_____

_____

_____

_____

_____

Letter to the Reader

Dear Reader,

You have created an opening for communication with God, Spirit, Source, the Universe, Life. New ideas and fresh, vibrant, life-giving thoughts will inspire you to act and live differently, which will attract new experiences and playing fields to you. You may be surprised at how much more there is to see and experience than what you currently know.

You may even begin to feel more alive, more youthful and more yourself again. *Feeling more* is the result of the time you invest in building your spiritual muscles. As new life comes in, old stuff we once believed comes up to be addressed and put to rest. This makes room for something new and more wonderful to happen.

Go with it. Go with the flow of it. Seek help if needed to support yourself and what is being birthed in you. You are worth it. You are most definitely worth investing in. That spark of light has been lit, fired up in you. Watch out, world! You are being born anew.

Desires that you never thought possible are now looking like they are attainable. Your energy level is up. There is a new excitement for life. Your vibration is high. You now have the energy to take on projects or new endeavors that you didn't have before in your survival mode of existence. Something has been freed up in you and now you are ready.

New, creative ideas cause you to burst with energy and break new ground. Things begin to show up in the outer world that weren't there before, matching up with the new going on inside you.

There will always be some fine tuning involved on this journey. There will always be more being revealed as you go along. The beautiful thing about spiritual practices is that you can't really do them wrong if your intention is in the right place and you come to them with as much of an open mind and heart as you can muster.

Just working with one or two of your favorite exercises and incorporating them into your daily life can make all the difference. They will help strengthen and fortify you and bring out the best in you...more than you ever realized was there.

As you incorporate more of these exercises throughout your day, you will find that you have set up enjoyable rituals that can keep you on track and remind you that you have an ongoing, reliable relationship with an incredibly amazing Universe which only continues to get better and better with each day. Learning to work with Life and being an expression of Life yourself is an adventure beyond words. Knowing yourself in a greater way and seeing what you can do is satisfying and fulfilling at such a deep level. It is from these experiences that you will be richly fed. This kind of spiritual sustenance can carry you through even the most difficult of times and help you create a life that is more to your preferred specifications.

As you go along, you will see how beautifully your practices blend together with your new way of being, resulting in an extraordinary life. You may want to shout from the mountaintops how great all of this is and how magnificent it is for you to be creating with and as the God within you. However, it is best to discuss new projects with only one or two close people who will not try to talk you out of it and will see that this is something very special and precious... the divine process of creation working through you and all around you. After all, there is indeed something new and wonderful that you are giving birth to: the Real You!

It will be hard for others not to notice a difference in you. Some may be excited to follow suit themselves. Be sure to share what is happening with only those who can appreciate what is going on and who love and support you. Those who want the highest and best for us are people we can trust. Others may not understand or be ready to appreciate these things yet.

Your spiritual practices will help you stay grounded and standing on a firm foundation. They are essential, especially for those times of huge shifts that shake the ground you walk on.

Take care of yourself in these ways and you will always be guided and protected.

You are amazing! You are like a new plant breaking through the tough ground. Soon you will be strong enough to stand on your own and face the world. In this time of much change and growth, expansion and transformation, we must all keep on going, for it *will* only get better and better if we will, *ad infinitum!*

It truly is a wonderful world once you know that who you are is more than you appear to be, more than this body, mind, life and experiences. Beginning to see yourself as spirit is quite a realization. Once you know that this is a friendly Universe that is always on your side, once you know how IT works and how to work with IT, this Power and Presence will do whatever you want as long as you come from love.

Does it get any better than that?

Knowing the highest and best for you and yours, always!

Namaste'
Cath

We need fear nothing in the Universe. We need not be afraid of God. We may be certain that all will arrive at the final goal that not one will be missing. Every man is an incarnation of God. The soul can no more be lost than God could be lost. We should neither be disturbed by the wailing of prophets, nor the anathemas of theology. We cannot believe that because we have subscribed to some creed, we have thereby purchased a seat in heaven, nor can we believe in any vindictive or malicious power in the universe, which damns us because we have erred through human ignorance. We believe in God and that He is Good. What more can life demand of us than that we do the best that we can and try to improve? If we have done this, we have done well and all will be right with our souls both here and hereafter. This leaves us free to work out our own salvation—not with fear or even with trembling—but with peace and in quiet confidence.

~ Ernest Holmes

Appendices

There are many kinds of Spiritual Practices. On the following pages are forms for
1. The Ideal Day,
2. Mind Treatment,
3. Sacred Space Covenant,
4. Sacred Covenant,
5. Timeline Questions,
6. Spiritual Autobiography Questions.

Make copies for yourself. Once you have the form memorized, you can write it from memory in your journal or vary it in any way that suits you.

Ideal Day

Date: _____

My ideal day is filled with:

_____

_____

_____

_____

I AM:

_____

_____

_____

_____

SPIRIT, Source, or Universe, in me and around me, I am ready to experience the following:

_____

_____

_____

_____

MAKE IT SO in a special way that only you can.

I follow my inner guidance and take the next action steps I know to take:

1. _____

_____

2. _____

_____

3. _____

_____

4. _____

_____

5. _____

_____

I AM grateful for:

_____

_____

_____

_____

I AM grateful for highest and best happening for (others):

_____

_____

_____

_____

I WHOLEHEARTEDLY ACCEPT ALL THIS and MORE.

AND SO IT IS!

Mind Treatment

Topic or Desire (What you want to do, have or be):

_____

_____

_____

Recognition (There's only one creative power, everywhere equally present)

_____

_____

_____

_____

_____

_____

_____

Unification (I am... embodying those same attributes)

_____

_____

_____

_____

_____

_____

_____

Affirmation/Realization (That which I desire has already been given)

_____

_____

_____

_____

_____

_____

_____

Denial (Anything unlike what I desire has no power in itself or in my life)

_____
_____
_____
_____
_____
_____
_____

Reaffirmation (So I can have it)

_____
_____
_____
_____
_____
_____
_____

Gratitude (I'm grateful to know it)

_____
_____
_____
_____
_____
_____
_____

Release (I don't have to know how to do it, I let go, let God figure out the how)

_____
_____
_____
_____
_____
_____

And so it is!

Sacred-Space Covenant

Our Covenant: (describe the group and its intention)

_____

_____

I agree to:

_____

_____

I agree to:

_____

_____

I agree to:

_____

_____

I agree to:

_____

_____

I use as my guide: If it is loving, if it grows, expands or deepens love, it's the right thing to do! (Or, in your own words):

_____

_____

_____

_____

Signed _____

Date_____

Sacred Covenant

(Why am I here?) I AM HERE TO:

_____
_____

(I AM Statements or affirmations) I AM:

_____
_____
_____
_____

(Daily agreements &commitments) I AGREE TO:

_____
_____
_____
_____

THE UNIVERSE AGREES TO:

_____
_____

(Gratitude statement) I AM GRATEFUL FOR:

_____
_____
_____
_____

(Dedications) I DEDICATE MY LIFE TO:

_____
_____
_____

THE UNIVERSE DEDICATES ITS LIFE TO:

_____
_____

(Closing) AND SO IT IS!

Timeline Questions

What key events influenced my life?

    1. _____

    2. _____

    3. _____

    4. _____

What was I going through at the time and how did I feel about it?

_____

_____

_____

_____

How did I resolve or get over a life challenge?

_____

_____

_____

_____

Is there a pattern in my life that becomes clear?

_____

_____

_____

_____

Who were some of the important people in my life?

    1. _____

    2. _____

    3. _____

    4. _____

What gifts did they give me?

    1. _____

    2. _____

    3. _____

    4. _____

What drastic or upsetting changes took place in my life?

_____

_____

_____

_____

What moments were eye openers that I will never forget?

_____

_____

_____

_____

What experiences really caused me to grow?

_____

_____

_____

_____

What moves did I make in my life and how did they change me?

_____

_____

_____

_____

What upsets took place that were unexpected?

_____

_____

_____

_____

What plans or changes took place that were "supposed" to happen?

_____

_____

_____

_____

Keep in mind that this might be interesting for others to find after we are gone. Even the challenges or incomplete parts may touch those close to us and help them to see us as relatable. Maybe our loved ones are going through similar difficulties and/or landmark occasions to celebrate.

Spiritual Autobiography Questions

Who were the key players in my life?

_____
_____
_____
_____

Who were the people who influenced my thinking and what I value today?

_____
_____
_____
_____

What events, circumstances and situations happened that helped make me who I am today?

_____
_____
_____
_____

Who were my teachers, my spiritual leaders and mentors, writers that touched me and helped me think and grow?

_____
_____
_____
_____

Who were the strangers that said something to me that I will never forget?

_____
_____

_____
_____

How has my concept of God changed through the years? What was my first idea of God and how has it evolved over the years?

_____
_____
_____
_____

What is it now?

_____
_____
_____
_____

What would I like it to be?

_____
_____
_____
_____

What shifts took place in my thinking that turned things around for me?

_____
_____
_____
_____

What gifts came out of the difficult years?

_____
_____
_____
_____

What did I do that really made me happy?

_____

_____

_____

_____

What has brought me to the point where I am now on my spiritual path?

_____

_____

_____

_____

Further questions to ask:

What's calling me now?

_____

_____

_____

_____

What am I going to find or what am I hoping to find when I answer that call?

_____

_____

_____

_____

Acknowledgements

To Central Florida Center for Spiritual Living for our 25 years together growing, evolving and expanding...the consciousness we developed together was incredible and the sacred community we created was out of this world! For that experience, which grew me exponentially, I am forever grateful to you all!

To clients I was honored to work with individually, who wanted more intensive work on themselves, I am thankful to have been invited into their personal space to support them even more, spiritually. I can't tell you how much fabulous growth I was privileged to be a part of. I grew even more because of our work, which gave me more love and understanding to share with the world.

To my family who continue to love and support me...each in their own special way. To cousin Walter, who introduced me to not only Science of Mind but the Abraham teachings as well, and who continues to be my cheerleader.

To Colette, my oldest and closest friend from childhood, for going through the book twice and making suggestions...most of all for still being in my life, sticking with me through thick and thin!

To Jeannie and Chris Zokan, my cousins, for being readers and lovingly supporting our work all these years. So lovely knowing you are always there.

To Nicole, my beautiful niece, who wrote me an encouraging note after book #1 saying she wanted more, and for doing a final run through this book. I can't thank you enough for urging me on.

To Cynder, my long-time friend, still with me, who used to pass me good spiritual books to read in the early days. Thank you, Cynder, for critiquing the book and pointing out places where I needed to be clearer so that this work could reach a larger audience.

To Carol, another very close friend who joined me on this spiritual adventure 30 years ago and who is always there for me. Thank you, Carol, for being a reader and for all the encouragement you continue to give.

To Sheryl, a beautiful friend and spirit, whom I have known since our boys were in kindergarten and are now beautiful young men. Thank you, Sheryl, for being the main editor and helping my work take shape – not only clarifying concepts, but with all the detail work. I can't thank you enough.

To Sam Goff, my prayer treatment partner and longtime friend of 19 years, my confessor who regularly keeps me on track with the highest and most loving consciousness always.

To Rev. Karen Wolfson, for being my first practitioner, who is responsible for this wonderful guy I married and who continues to love and support me.

To my children, Nick, Liz and Joseph, and my 3-year old twin granddaughters, Aubrey and Everly, who have enriched my life immensely. They all keep me young at heart and continuously evolving.

To my husband, John, who faithfully stands by my side no matter what... a strong, loving, spiritual partner that I have been blessed with for almost 30 years.

Thank you so much Rev. Ruth Miller, Ph.D. for working on the finishing touches, (and on the title). All making the book extra special. I am honored by your gorgeous assistance and endorsement.

Thank you to Doug Hay, the sculptor, who so graciously shared a picture of his Heron masterpiece on the front cover.

To Michael Terranova, Publisher at Wise Woman Press, I can't thank you enough for taking on my second book, suggesting it become a workbook, and for working with me and for me to make my way easy. You are a godsend!

This has most definitely been a group project of love. I could not have completed this project without everyone playing their part. Thank you from the bottom of my heart! I love our creation and know it is filled with spiritual treasures for all who are ready. I can't tell you what you mean to me!

About the Author

Cath DePalma, a pioneer in the study of metaphysics, has dedicated her life to working with universal principles and practicing how they work in real-life situations. She has a great understanding of how Life works and what is needed to experience the greatest possible results. It is from her own life lessons, discoveries, years of life experiences, and expertise that she teaches and guides others in a fun, loving way that inspires and empowers them to experiment with these principles in their own lives.

For the past 27 years she has counseled, coached and encouraged thousands of people from all over the world with different backgrounds and beliefs. Cath and her husband, John, co-directed the Central Florida Center for Spiritual Living (a Science of Mind center in Orlando) for 25 years. A motivational speaker, teacher and writer, Cath has a unique gift for working with others as they move through transformation in their lives. She is the author of *I Can Do This Thing Called Life and So Can You!* and now, its beautiful companion workbook, *Energize Your Creative Super Powers.* Currently, she is available for speaking, workshops, and private consultations.

Contact Cath DePalma by email:
cdepalma@ticl.org

Books Published by WiseWoman Press

By Emma Curtis Hopkins

- *Resume*
- *The Gospel Series*
- *Class Lessons of 1888*
- *Self Treatments including The Radiant I Am*
- *High Mysticism*
- *Genesis Series 1894*
- *Esoteric Philosophy Deeper Teachings in Spiritual Science*
- *Drops of Gold Journal*
- *Judgment Series in Spiritual Science*
- *Bible Interpretations: Series I, thru XXII*

By Ruth L. Miller

- *Unveiling Your Hidden Power: Emma Curtis Hopkins' Metaphysics for the 21st Century*
- *Coming into Freedom: Emily Cady's Lessons in Truth for the 21st Century*
- *Power Beyond Magic: Ernest Holmes Biography*
- *Power to Heal: Emma Curtis Hopkins Biography*
- *The Power of Unity: Charles Fillmore Biography*
- *Power of Thought: Phineas P. Quimby Biography*
- *The Power of Insight: Thomas Troward Biography*
- *The Power of the Self: Ralph Waldo Emerson Biography.*
- *The Power of Practice: Emily Cady Biography)*

By Frances B. Lancaster

- *The 13th Commandment*
- *Abundance Now*

By Christine Green

- *Authentic Spirituality – A Woman's Guide to Living An Empowered Life*
- *A Caregivers Journal*

By Cath DePalma

- *I Can Do This Thing Called Life And So Can You*

Made in the USA
Columbia, SC
31 July 2020